BONSAI

BONSAI

Constance Tindale

The Crowood Press

First published in 2001 by
The Crowood Press Ltd
Ramsbury, Marlborough
Wiltshire SN8 2HR

British Library Cataloguing-in-Publication Data
A catalogue record for this book is available from the British Library.

ISBN 1 86126 418 6

Photograph previous page: Wat Phu Temple, in Champansak, Laos, SE Asia: while trees colonize every nook and cranny in the brickwork, small metallic 'bonsai' Trees-of-Life have been offered to these Buddha images in the ruins of the thousand-year-old temple

Photographic Acknowledgements
Photographs of the Bonsai Centre and of the trees in Lodders, the Netherlands, by David Shearwood; photographs of Bonsai Centres in Japan and of Japanese-trained trees by Andy Tennent; photographs of Bryce Canyon, USA, by Samantha Tindale. All other photographs by the author.

Line illustrations by Cy Baker

Typeset by
Florence Production Ltd, Stoodleigh, Devon
Printed and bound in Singapore by
Craft Print International Ltd

Dedication
This book is dedicated to tree lovers throughout the world, and to my daughter Sam who for years accompanied me around the Chelsea Flower Show in the rain – may your leaves be as green as your fingers.

Acknowledgements
Without the help of my family, bonsai-loving friends and the staff at Crowood it would have been impossible for me to write this book. Special thanks go to Andy Tennant of Norfolk, for access to his trees and for his photos of Japanese trees, and to Alan Lavender and David Shearwood for their friendship, for sharing their knowledge, for encouraging me for years and for access to their trees. Thanks also to Graham Potter, Graham Benefer, Stuart Norris, Brian Carver and Diana White of Norfolk Bonsai Association, for allowing access to their trees; to Keith Howard of Anglia Bonsai for encouragement and advice; to Samantha Tindale and Monaghan Tindale, for taking photographs of trees in outlandish places and for generally waiting for their meals for most of their lives while the kitchen was half-filled with bonsai trees; to Mick Tindale for making most of my pots, tolerating my obsession, allowing me to use his hands in photographs and for watering my trees while I live in a desert; and to Egyptian friends who have listened to me moan about living in said desert and who have tried unrelentingly to prevent the goats from eating my embryonic garden. Everything you all did was truly appreciated.

Contents

Contents

Styled trees in a Japanese bonsai centre: a rock-planted group of Japanese White Pines (ABOVE) and a slab-planted group of junipers (RIGHT)

Preface

The fact that you're reading this introduction means that you already have an interest in trees, and I don't need to convince you of their beauty. Bonsai trees enable you to enjoy that beauty at close quarters and to use your artistic talents and horticultural skills to create your own living masterpiece. A bonsai tree needs care in the same way that any other living part of your household does and it will take equally as much time and patience for you to achieve a desired outcome as training a puppy would. Describing a bonsai as a 'tree in a pot' does not even start to do justice to the art of bonsai design, but it does give an idea of how the bonsai should be nurtured.

When I first became interested in bonsai, photographs of 500-year-old trees from national collections were awe-inspiring but made me feel inadequate. I knew that I would never be able to develop trees like that myself and would never be rich enough to buy them from someone else. Some time later I learned that the trees I admired so much were actually Imperial sixteen-handers; they were up to 10ft (3m) tall, in enormous pots, and needed eight strong-armed men to move them. I stopped longing to own one myself and, although I still admired the power of these huge trees, I became content with owning small two-handers that I could pick up and move about without having to hire a crane.

People are drawn to bonsai from several standpoints. There are those who have artistic ability and wish to apply it to a living thing but need to learn about horticulture; others are used to growing things but need to learn more about art and design. The former may have the advantage while training the tree, but the latter definitely have the upper hand in keeping it alive. I had worked for years in commercial market gardening and amateur garden design. Consequently, my fears were not to do with watering, re-potting and survival; rather, I was concerned about which branches I should cut off my beloved tree to enhance its appearance. I broke into a cold sweat each time I closed the cutters and watched a branch fall, knowing that I could never restore the severed limb. Like everyone, I suffered disasters and fatalities, but over the years I learned that by applying basic rules I could minimize my losses and end up with an admirable collection of beautiful healthy miniature trees.

Visitors tend to ask the same questions about my trees: 'How old are they?', 'How do you keep them alive?' and 'How do you keep them small?' They sometimes add, sadly, 'I had one once but it died. I'd like to try again but they are so difficult and so expensive.' When I ask them what type of tree they had they usually reply, 'It was a small one.'

Bonsai trees are small, but they aren't difficult and, if you develop them yourself, they need not be expensive either. Newcomers to the art are usually more concerned, however, about the tree's survival than its development. Ironically, they are more likely to kill a tree with kindness than with neglect, especially if they have already suffered a tree fatality.

By the way, my answer to the age question is, 'How old does it look?'

My aim for this manual is to pass on to the enthusiastic beginner my knowledge of the basic skills needed to identify, care for and refine bonsai trees. I also want to explain techniques by which bonsai trees can be created from cuttings, garden-centre stock or collected material. I have used photographs of trees in their natural habitats, to illustrate how trees grow in different environments, as well as some inspirational photographs of extensively trained bonsai, to encourage the development of higher skills. However, as this is intended to be a practical manual, most of the bonsai trees shown are either mine, or owned by ordinary Bonsai Club Members. Many of these trees have forgivable faults, but they show the sort of results that can be achieved in a relatively short time, and at low cost, using the basic skills described. I have focused on the beginner, but there is information within this manual that will be helpful to bonsai enthusiasts of all levels of expertise.

A selection of case histories shows trees that have progressed from 'sow's ears'. They are not yet 'silk purses' but they are on their way, given a couple of decades. They were chosen because they were at times considered beyond hope of becoming 'proper' bonsai trees. All were developed from garden-centre trees or collected material and, at various times, were very nearly relegated to the compost heap.

For the warmest half of the year I live in a small village in England and for the coldest part of the British winter I decamp to an even smaller village in Egypt. I have yet to try and raise bonsai trees in a desert but as the ancient Egyptians managed to grow trees in pots I just might give it a try – goats permitting. Meanwhile, my trees in England are entrusted to the winter care of a Heath-Robinson watering system and an overburdened family, all of whom are thriving.

Connie Tindale
September 2000

Bonsai flourished in the Far East, with different styles being developed in each country: bonsai trees at the Reunification Palace, Saigon, Vietnam (ABOVE) and at the Wat Po Temple in Bangkok

I
Knowing the Tree

1 The Art and History of Bonsai

What is bonsai and when did it start? Although we know what bonsai is, a question mark will always remain over its origins. The ancients believed that the spirit of the tree was extremely powerful, and treated trees with reverence and religious awe; surely they would have kept one close to the home? What is sure about bonsai's history is that the highly developed art that we recognize today owes both its name and its rules to Japan. Even though Japan is not where the art of bonsai started, no other country has devoted such time and patience to the miniaturization and styling of trees.

A bonsai tree is a living thing. As such, it is never finished and will require care and attention throughout its entire life. If it is healthy, its lifespan may be much longer than that of any human since Methuselah. In Japan, a bonsai tree is a living family heirloom, passed from one generation to the next. Since Sotheby's auction house has sold bonsai collections alongside antiques and fine art, trees in Britain have also moved into this category. However, even a classic tree costing thousands of pounds

needs the same care as any other bonsai tree; if it isn't pruned, it will lose its shape; if it isn't watered, it will die. Whatever the carer does to the tree is reflected in the way it looks. It will never be complete, but it will reward its creator

Spirit of the tree – Northern Thailand: a forest shrine stands next to a tree wrapped in prayer cloths

LEFT: *Japanese-styled tree – Trident Maple (Acer buergerianum): this beautiful old tree has been given great care and has been regularly pruned into its wonderful shape*

RIGHT: *Thai-style garden at Wat Po Temple, Bangkok: highly trained trees make up this fantastical garden landscape and further highlight the difference between Japanese and Thai methods of styling trees*

Japanese-style garden at Chelsea Flower Show: bonsai techniques have been applied to the styling of these trees, enabling the power and grace of a fully grown tree to be shown in a small space

ten times over for the time and attention to detail that is lavished upon it.

What aspect of bonsai drew you to the art? Was it the grace of the tree or its power? Do small trees evoke in you a feeling of peace and serenity or an impression of power over nature? These are important questions, as the answers will lead you towards the style of tree that will bring you the most enjoyment. The art of bonsai should never be a chore. Above all else, in keeping with the spirit of the tree, bonsai should bring pleasure to those who create them and those who care for them.

Different cultures have produced differently styled trees. The Japanese style of training trees is very different from that of the Chinese, whose style is again different from that found in the other countries of Asia and the Far East. The Japanese style is one of the most pleasing to the eye – it aims to give a more natural representation of a mature tree – but no style is superior to another; they are simply different. Over the centuries the Japanese have developed sets of 'rules' to govern what is considered to be a classic bonsai tree. These rules are guidelines only. A tree really only has to please its carer and creator.

The skills of the Japanese masters were not confined to bonsai. They also applied their techniques to glorious effect on trees trained for spectacular garden settings. The trees were not turned into spiral shapes or made to look like animals, as in topiary, but were carefully studied so that their natural beauty was enhanced with careful pruning. In this way, the power and grace of fully-grown trees could be displayed in a tiny courtyard setting as well as in pots. In Thailand, too, styled trees are used to great effect in the gardens of many temples.

The Art of Bonsai

The word 'bonsai' is made up of two other Japanese words: *bon* meaning tree and *sai*

meaning pot or tray. Bonsai is, therefore, by definition simply a 'tree in a pot' or a 'tree on a tray'. In practice, it is a complex and highly developed art form, rather than a simple horticultural practice.

A mature tree has certain characteristics: it has surface roots that anchor and buttress it against inclement weather; it has a trunk that is somewhat gnarled, thick at the bottom but getting thinner towards the top; and its branches have been weighed down by leaves and the passing of time. Whether it is a pine, oak, maple, magnolia, rowan or a Christmas tree, if it is mature it will carry the marks of its age and have a character of its own. The art of bonsai is to apply special techniques that will reproduce these characteristics in a tree that is small enough to plant in a pot. It does not involve magic but it does involve illusion.

Like many other art forms, bonsai styling depends upon an *impression* of the tree rather than a photo-like reproduction. A bonsai tree should mirror the better points of its natural big brothers but should downplay their faults. Branches that cross, grow straight up or at odd angles that obscure the line of the trunk should be removed, allowing the line and taper of the trunk to be displayed. The part that horticulture plays in the process should not be underestimated; no matter how much 'art' is practised on the tree, unless it is healthy it will become a pallid imitation of what it is meant to be. It takes time and patience to turn a 'stick in a pot' or a 'stump in a bucket' into a 'tree on a tray'.

The special relationship between a mature bonsai and its container is very important. A tree brought home from the garden centre for

planting in the garden is a tree in a pot, but it certainly could not be described as a bonsai tree. Shape, depth, colour and glaze are all factors to be taken into account when choosing a pot for a particular tree. A very small bonsai tree planted in a very large pot, for example, has a limited impact, as the tree and the pot do not relate to each other. Combining the two to the greatest effect is a major part of the art.

While a tree is young and in training it should not be in a bonsai pot at all, but planted

TOP LEFT: *This is a tree in a pot, but is it a bonsai? For details on this tree's development towards being a bonsai, see Chapter 15*

TOP MIDDLE AND RIGHT: *The trunks of mature trees have character and show the marks of their age. As a result of its environment, the trunk of this stunted pine (*MIDDLE*) is gnarled and twisted. The trunk and roots of this ancient hawthorn (*RIGHT*) have the characteristics that bonsai attempts to emulate*

Blickling Park, Norfolk: Mother Nature does not always make good bonsai trees – the branches of this massive oak tree are growing in all directions

TOP LEFT: *Japanese Maple (Acer palmatum): this chumono maple is only 20in (50cm) high and represents a natural tree rather than mirroring one*

LOWER LEFT: *Japanese Black Pine (Pinus thunbergii), approximately 75 years old and 24in (60cm) high*

TOP RIGHT: *Detail from the trunk of the pine: the tree has a dramatic trunk with an interesting twist and mature bark*

- to create an illusion;
- to bring the countryside into the home;
- to re-create and refine nature; and
- to capture the spirit of the tree, keeping it close while reflecting on its exquisite beauty.

The History of Bonsai

Egypt

The earliest record of pot-planted trees is shown in the tombs of the Valley of the Kings at Luxor in Egypt. Care of the kings' estates was handed over to their ministers (viziers); Rekhmire and Sennefer are the most famous of these, renowned for the lavish decoration of their final resting-places. In the dark unilluminated recesses of Rekhmire's tomb, wall paintings describe a vizier's duties in caring for the Pharaoh's estates, including his tree-lined gardens. Sennefer illustrated his position as caretaker of the Pharaoh's wine supply by decorating his tomb with paintings of grapes and vine leaves. On one of the tomb's supporting pillars is a painting of a table on which someone is hiding in the foliage of a tree growing from a small pot. A symbolic gesture or an embryonic bonsai?

Nearly 4,000 years ago, Rekhmire and then Sennefer were viziers first to Tutmose III, who for many years was usurped by his stepmother Hatshepsut, and then to Amenophis II. Although the vengeful Tutmose had all references to Hatshepsut destroyed, her fabulous temple still stands, built on rock at the base of

in something much bigger where it can stretch and grow.

One misconception about bonsai trees is that they take a long time to grow. They may take a long time to mature, as that is in the nature of the tree, but a healthy well-nourished tree grows furiously and needs almost constant pruning and trimming during the summer months to control its upward surge. The Japanese have excelled in the skills of control, pruning and shaping, producing trees that are visual masterpieces of power and grace.

In summary, the art of bonsai has a number of aims:

a mountain. It is known to have had wonderful gardens, with terraces of solid stone; surely most of the trees would have been in pots and controlled by regular pruning? They may not have been bonsai as we know it today but the concept is similar.

China

In China, trees were considered to be the link between heaven and earth. For millennia it was customary to plant pines and cypresses (thought to have greater vitality than others) on graves, to strengthen the soul of the departed and to save the body from corruption. The trees were subsequently thought to encompass the soul of the deceased.

Although the first example of a potted tree might have come from Egypt, the first recognizable record of the art of bonsai comes from Xian in China. Again, it is in the form of a tomb painting, on the wall of the tomb of Zhang Huai, second son of the Empress. The 2,000-year-old mural depicts a servant carrying a bonsai tree.

The art was known as *pen-tsai*, which has the same meaning and sounds very similar to *bonsai*. At this stage, trees were collected from the wild and planted in decorative pots in their natural form. In the ink-wash paintings of the

Wall paintings from tombs in Luxor, Egypt. One painting from the tomb of Rekhmire (RIGHT) shows men at work in Pharaoh's gardens; it was painted nearly 4,000 years ago. The painting from the tomb of Sennefer (LEFT), shows a potted shrub on a table

The Art and History of Bonsai

TOP LEFT: *Chinese temple, Kuala Lumpur, West Malaysia: azaleas and other bonsai trees are used to decorate Buddhist temples*

TOP RIGHT: *Bonsai trees at Wat Po Temple, Bangkok: Thai trees were often pruned to represent a magical symbol evoking a human character trait*

LOWER LEFT: *Rock-planted tree on the terrace of the Reunification Palace, Saigon, Vietnam: Vietnamese bonsai trees are more free in style than Japanese trees. This rock-planted tree is in a magnificent antique red pot*

LOWER RIGHT: *Vientiane, Laos: straggly bonsai trees compete for light with a demon in a shady corner of the Buddha Park*

Sung Dynasty (AD960–1280), artists represented whole landscapes with a few brush strokes, and many painted trees that had been naturally stunted and transplanted into pots. Other paintings show that it was not until centuries later that pruning techniques were applied and forms that we would recognize as bonsai began to emerge.

Pen-tsai was a pastime reserved for the rich, who had the time to devote to their trees and the resources both for buying pots and for sending out collecting parties to find trees that had been naturally stunted by harsh conditions. During the Ming Dynasty (AD1368–1644), renowned for its fabulous vases, a glorious marriage was forged between collected trees and spectacular pots. A general love of nature and reverence for trees led not only to the collection of single trees, but also the creation of miniature landscapes, or *pen-tsing*, using rocks, small buildings and even figurines. Rocks represented mountains, sand represented water and dwarfed trees represented the link between heaven and earth.

Representations of Thai signs from the K'long-Tamra el Mat, a nineteenth-century treatise on trees: a. The Curtain; b. The Dancer; c. Physical Strength; d. The Obsequious Person

a. b. c. d.

With the increase in trading, the practice began to flourish in all nearby countries where there were large Chinese communities and during the seventeenth century the art ceased to be a pastime only of the nobility and became accessible to everyone.

South-East Asia

In the countries of South-East Asia, where the sanctity of trees is still recognized, bonsai developed in a different way. In Thailand, bonsai trees became highly stylized and single trees were pruned into magical symbols. These symbols were evocative both of tangible things (for example, the forest) and of human character traits, such as cunning and mischief-making. A record of the styles is given is the *Klong-Tamra Mai-Dat*, a treatise on the tree written by a Thai poet in the nineteenth century. A number of the tree styles are represented in the drawings on page 14. Evidence of these styles can still be seen in the trees of the Wat Po Temple in Bangkok. Indeed, it is difficult to separate bonsai from religion, as it is in the temples of South-East Asia that the majority of bonsai trees are to be found.

In Vietnam, bonsai trees were considered to be the bearers of mans' misfortunes. In Laos, Cambodia and Malaysia, styling was completed primarily by pruning rather than wiring and, as in China, the spirit of the tree was allowed to follow its own path.

Japan

Bonsai centre, Japan

With the rise of Zen, it is likely that Buddhist monks brought bonsai trees to Japan from China in the twelfth century. Although Buddhism is basically a non-theistic religion, the monks regarded trees as a sacred link between God and mankind and would have taken their trees with them when moving to Japan. The teachings of Zen were concerned with stripping away all that was unnecessary in life. Gone was decoration for its own sake. Japanese gardeners sought to create gardens that reflected the minimalist ink-wash paintings of the Chinese Sung Dynasty; they provided an ideal background for trees that had been naturally dwarfed by the Japanese landscape.

BOTTOM LEFT: A magnificent styled tree awaits new owners in a bonsai centre in Japan RIGHT: The serenity evoked by this juniper, together with the water bowl, is timeless

Bonsai centre, Lodders, Netherlands

The Japanese applied their mastery of miniaturization not only to trees and gardens, but also to paintings, ceramics and other art forms. Many theories have been put forward to explain this love of tiny things. The most logical theory – and also the most recent – arises from the findings of research into eyesight. Seventy-five per cent of the adult population of Japan have been found to be myopic, experiencing difficulty in focusing on distant objects but being able to see very small objects with great clarity. Ceramics were highly advanced in Japan but sight-correcting glass lenses were not available in the country until they began to be imported in the mid-nineteenth century.

As in China, the art of bonsai in Japan was initially reserved for the aristocracy, the Samurai, but interest spread to the affluent 'upper classes' and then to the general population. Eventually it was a hobby that was participated in at all levels of Japanese society. In the late nineteenth century Japan sent trees to France for the World Fair, but it was several decades before the start of a flourishing export trade began. Today Japanese trees are recognized as being special and are exported to all parts of the world.

Later, in the mid-seventeenth century, it is known that a Chinese official fleeing to Japan, to escape the Manchus, brought with him all his literature pertaining to *pen-tsai* cultivation and training. It was from these writings that the Japanese art as we know it developed. Although the Japanese became masters at styling and training trees, their results were achieved through careful selective pruning. It was not until about a century ago that wire was first used to bend branches and hold them to shape.

Europe

From the Middle Ages onwards, the British were avid plant collectors, with explorers travelling the world to find specimen trees, plants and shrubs to grace the purpose-built conservatories and elaborate gardens of stately homes. Although many of these trees were pot-planted for transportation, and fruit-bearing trees such as lemons and oranges were grown in pots in beautiful orangeries, the idea was not to keep them small, but to encourage them to grow as big as possible.

Bonsai reached Europe from China in the fourteenth century, as exploration expanded and interest in the oriental arts became fashionable. By the eighteenth century, sailors returning from various European colonies had brought back examples of bonsai as curios for collectors, gardeners and apothecaries. It was a passing fancy and interest waned fairly rapidly, probably because the trees' owners lacked the skills to keep them healthy. In addition, until relatively recent times, Europe was densely forested. Just a couple of centuries ago, it was said that a squirrel

Bryce Canyon, USA: conifers have managed to find a foothold even in the most inhospitable part of this canyon

could travel from one end of Warwickshire to another without touching the ground. The tree was revered in spiritual terms, but did not have the same curiosity value as it did in those countries with a harsher climate and topography, or where space was limited.

In 1878, bonsai were brought from Japan for public display at the World Fair in Paris, and more bonsai trees were shown at an exhibition in London in 1909. At first, the bonsai trees and miniature landscapes failed once again to thrive, as they had in earlier times; the belief was that some degree of magic must have been used by the Japanese in order to control the growth of the trees.

Interest was revived between the First and Second World Wars, but waned again in the 1940s and 50s. It was a time when the Japanese bonsai traditions were largely ignored and British bonsai developed a style of its own. Some say that this was detrimental to the art, but styling is often dictated by climate as well as culture and, out of respect for the spirit of the tree, British style might be described as different but should not be described as worse.

Since the 1960s, with easier travel and communication, interest in the classical styles has grown. Now, in the early years of the twenty-

Bonsai club workshop: bonsai clubs are excellent places to get advice and learn new skills

first century, more and more information is available on ways in which bonsai trees should be grown and trained, and Europe is back on track in producing excellent trees.

Over the centuries, the art of bonsai has metamorphosed from dependence upon rich collectors of curios into a universal hobby. Clubs and societies all over the world encourage enthusiastic amateurs, organize demonstrations by professionals, and display trees of a high standard, making an invaluable contribution to the spread of the art.

2 Learning from Nature – How Trees Grow

It is easier to learn how to care for and develop a bonsai tree if there is some understanding of how it would grow in its natural habitat. In its most basic form, a bonsai is simply a tree in a pot. If the tree is to stay healthy and flourish, the conditions in which the tree would naturally grow need to be simulated as closely as possible. There are 60,000 to 70,000 existing different species of tree and all of them have evolved to live in slightly different conditions so that they are never in direct competition with each other, increasing the survival rate of each species. With patience and care, just about every species of tree could become bonsai. In practice, those with really large leaves can be problematic, as it is very difficult to reduce the leaf size so that is in scale with a miniaturized tree trunk.

To sustain life, whether in a pot or in the ground, a tree needs light, water and air. Using all three of these elements, and the process of photosynthesis, a tree is able to manufacture its own food, which is why evolution has enabled it to spend its whole life in one place. Being rooted to that spot does not mean that the tree is static; indeed, its leaves and branches move with grace and elegance.

Trees are the oldest living things on earth. Some of the giant redwoods of California are up to 3,000 years old, but the grand-daddies of all trees are the small, stunted bristlecone pines, which are thought to live up to 4,000 years. Some of today's bristlecone pines were already growing when the stones of Stonehenge formed

a complete circle and the wall paintings in the Valley of the Kings were still drying.

Not all trees are long-lived: the birch usually only manages around forty years before its demise, and the willow lives for even fewer years.

The most ancient of the tree species is the maidenhair tree, *Ginkgo biloba*, which has remained largely unchanged for over 200 million years. The ginkgo was considered to be a sacred tree by the Chinese and was able to survive from ancient times, carefully preserved in temple gardens. Without this special treatment, the species would probably have become extinct. (The gingko is rather unique in other ways, too: it is broad-leafed and deciduous, but has cones.)

Bonsai encompasses trees, shrubs and plants; the most popular are trees, because they usually have a longer lifespan. The difference between a tree and a shrub is commonly to be found in the stem. Normally, trees grow taller than shrubs and have a single woody trunk that has annual growth rings. Shrubs are usually much shorter and have multiple stems. Some species of smaller trees produce multiple trunks but it is not common to find a shrubby form of the larger species of trees.

Re-creation of the tree's natural habitat is achieved through the mix of the compost and the shape and depth of its pot. Compost mixes need to be more or less free-draining to reflect a particular tree's needs, and pots are shallower or deeper to reflect the tree's shape and root formation. As a guideline, in general terms:

Conifers in Bryce Canyon, USA (LEFT) and beeches in Thetford Forest, England (RIGHT): conifers have adapted to the harsh conditions of higher ground, whereas broadleaf trees prefer richer loam

- pines are found on rocky hillsides;
- junipers grow in wild exposed places;
- spruces grow in more boggy areas;
- large broad-leafed deciduous trees prefer the rich loam of valley bottoms; and
- azaleas and other flowering shrubs prefer the damp humus-rich acidic places under the tree canopy.

Deciduous or Evergreen?

Trees and shrubs fall into two groups: those that are deciduous and those that are evergreen. Evergreens keep most of their leaves all year, shedding only a few of the oldest leaves or needles and replacing them with new growth at the appropriate time for the climate in which they live. Deciduous trees lose all their leaves at some time of the year, usually just before the hardest season. In Europe, this is the coldest time of the year, but in other countries it could be either the driest or the darkest. Through evo-

lution, conifers have adapted to growing in the harsher conditions of higher ground whereas broadleaf trees prefer more congenial conditions.

Deciduous trees almost invariably have broad leaves but there are one or two species, the larch, for example, that have needles instead of broad leaves (which are still shed in the autumn). Whereas the majority of deciduous trees have the same general form of leaf, there are two distinctly different leaf forms to be found in evergreens. They have leaves that are either of the resinous needle type, which could be narrow or scale-like, or have broad leaves similar to the leaves of deciduous trees.

Many evergreen trees are softwoods, while deciduous trees tend to be hardwoods. The difference between the two becomes immediately apparent when working with them: softwoods are easy to bend, whereas the hardwoods are brittle, making them more durable but more difficult to manipulate. Softwoods usually end up in the saw mill, being pulped into paper and chipboard, while hardwoods are turned into furniture and long-lasting items of beauty.

Hillside scene created with stylized junipers

Basic Needs

Water

In times of drought, when water is severely restricted, the leaves on deciduous trees droop then dry, and are shed earlier than usual. Coniferous trees, and those that are used to growing at higher altitudes where rainfall is lower, do not show the same degree of distress when water is restricted. They are more resilient to drought conditions, although they will succumb eventually. In conifers, evidence of drought is shown through browning of the foliage rather than drooping leaves. Coniferous trees are usually shallow-rooted but oak trees have been known to send roots down more than 100ft (30m) to reach the water table.

In times of flood, the minute air pockets in the soil become permanently filled with water and air is prevented from reaching the tree's roots, causing them to rot. How much water a tree needs is dependent on its species but, over a period of time, too much water or too little water has the same ultimate outcome: the demise of the tree.

Over-watering, rather than under-watering, is a common problem in bonsai care and more trees die from root rot than from the effects of drought. However, with adequate drainage in the pot and a suitable free-draining compost mix, most trees will survive the over-enthusiastic waterer.

Light

Although the needles and leaves of trees need light to produce food, the roots and bark of the tree do not. Consequently, an evergreen tree will need light all year round, but a deciduous tree can manage without light during the winter months when it is devoid of leaves. Leaves do not appear in the middle of trees where outer growth restricts light access; in order to give a look of age, any inner leaves on bonsai trees are removed.

Trees are efficient mechanisms and will eliminate all those parts, roots or leaves that are not working as they should be. Placing the tree in a shady position to protect it from strong sunlight is beneficial, but severely restricting light or cutting out light completely will prevent the

leaves from doing their job. At first the growth will be pale and spindly but then the tree will discard all leaves that are not working efficiently; too many lost leaves could subsequently cause the tree to starve.

Lack of light leads to the inner parts of this cedar being devoid of needles

Air

Leaves need air for the process of photosynthesis. Without air the process cannot be accomplished and the tree will not receive the nourishment it needs. Air is also needed at the roots to prevent them from rotting and to assist the growth of the tree. If the compost in which the tree is growing is large grained and free draining then watering will force air down through the compost to the roots on a regular basis. If the compost is compacted, water will mainly run off and air will not penetrate as far down as the roots. However, large pockets of air that are devoid of soil mean there are areas where the tree's roots cannot draw up any water. As roots that are not serving a function will die back in the same way that leaves will, large air pockets must be eliminated when the tree is repotted (*see* Chapter 8).

Cut-Leafed Maples given the protection of a shady corner of the garden: while shade will protect a tree from strong sunlight, severely reduced light will cause leaves to die

The process of photosynthesis: trees are able to make their own food, which enables them to stay in one place

Leaves of oak (TOP RIGHT), field maple (MIDDLE RIGHT) and horse chestnut (LOWER RIGHT): the leaves of the oak tree are pinnate, the maple leaves are palmate, and those of the horse chestnut are compound

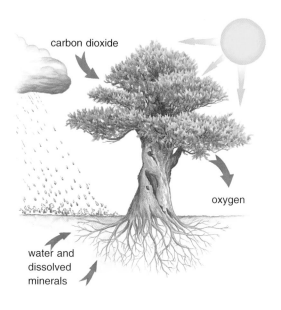

Leaves

Leaves, which are made up of a stem and a blade, are the principal food-making organs of the tree. Most leaf blades are of a green colour, caused by chlorophyll, which is a substance the

The red leaves of copper beech and pink, white and green leaves of a variegated butterfly maple: the maple leaves have areas that are devoid of chlorophyll, while those of the beech have extra pigments that allow other colours to be reflected

tree uses through the process of photosynthesis to manufacture carbohydrate sugars from water and carbon dioxide. The first step of photosynthesis is the absorption of light by the chlorophyll. Next, pores in the leaves extract carbon dioxide from the air and roots draw up water and dissolved minerals to complete a series of complex reactions that result in food being made and oxygen being released.

Some leaves, such as those of maples, have additional pigments that give them colour. Variegated leaves may have sections that are completely without pigments and chlorophyll, however there is always chlorophyll somewhere in the leaf, enabling it to produce food.

Pine needles (LEFT) and scales of juniper (MIDDLE): the shape of needles and scales is ideal for resisting cold drying winds

RIGHT: Foliage of the Gingko biloba, which has fern-like leaves and is the world's oldest species of tree

MIDDLE LEFT AND BELOW: Pigments in leaves break down as summer progresses: the blood-red leaves of this Japanese Maple deshojo turn increasingly pink and then green as the pigments break down and the chlorophyll begins to show through

The glorious riot of red, orange and gold leaves that is seen in the autumn is a result of the decomposition of the chlorophyll, which allows other pigments to be revealed.

Oak and beech trees have *simple* leaves – the overall shape differs, but each has a single un-divided blade with a central rib. Laburnum and horse chestnut have *compound* leaves, made up of several leaflets. A leaf that has a thick main rib running from its tip to its base is known as *pinnate*, while the leaf of a maple has several thick veins radiating out from its base and is known as *palmate*. An *Acer palmatum* 'Japoni-cum' is, therefore, a Japanese Maple with a leaf that has veins radiating out from the leaf's base rather than a single vein running along the leaf's length.

The shape and structure of a leaf is adapted to the conditions in which the tree lives. Most leaves are designed to expose as much of the leaf's surface to sunlight as possible, but

Annual growth rings on a severed branch from a Japanese flowering cherry tree – the diagonal lines are saw marks but the growth rings can be clearly seen and the difference between the light-coloured sapwood and the dark-coloured heartwood is quite clear

conifers, accustomed to cold, windy climates, have needle-like leaves that offer as little surface as possible to drying winds. Needles are of a different shape from bladed leaves but they serve exactly the same function. The leaves of trees from really arid regions are spongy so that a lot of moisture can be retained; leaves of tropical trees, on the other hand, have evolved in order to shed excess water. The spines of many plants, such as the hawthorn tree and the berberis shrub, are actually modified leaves, and the tendrils of climbing plants are undeveloped blades.

The way in which the leaves are arranged and how they are attached to the stem can also vary according to tree species. If more than two leaves are attached to the stem at the same level they are *whorled*. If two leaves are directly facing each other they are *opposite*; if they are arranged singly and spirally around the stem they are described as *alternate*.

Nutritional Delivery System

There are two types of tissue inside the tree, which make up the *vascular system* that transports water, minerals and food. The *xylem* conducts water and minerals from the ground to the stems and leaves, and the *phloem* distributes the food that has been produced in the leaves to the stems, roots and fruit. In general terms, the leaf is a food-producing factory, the xylem brings in some of the raw materials that are needed to make food, and the phloem carts the food off to where it is needed most. All of this is going on just under the bark; the *heartwood* in the middle of the tree is lifeless. That is why hollow oaks can continue to live for centuries without any centre and why insects that burrow just under the bark of the tree can cause so much damage.

In order to stay close to the bark the xylem and phloem need to renew annually. The annual renewal of this system leads to the growth rings in the trunk of the tree. From the size of these rings it is possible to detect whether it was a good or bad year for the development of the tree, and the number of rings indicates its age.

Roots

The root of a tree serves two functions: it anchors the tree to the ground and it also draws up water and dissolved minerals, which the tree is able to convert into nourishment. Roots, therefore, are usually underground and conform to the law of gravity by growing downwards. Underground, the tree roots are constantly spreading outwards to the edge of the canopy and downwards towards a water table in search for water. Only the fine hairs on the very tips of the roots take up moisture, so they need perpetually to renew themselves by extending.

Bonsai trees are confined to shallow pots, and their roots need regular pruning to encourage the proliferation of these fine root hairs and to maintain a greater density of roots near the trunk of the tree. Some trees, such as willows, root easily, which is why it is simple to propagate them from cuttings and air layering. Others, such as pines, seldom root without special treatment. The application of synthetic indoleacetic acid, in the form of rooting liquids and powders, can help stimulate the rooting process.

In its natural state, a tree has long taproots that anchor it in place. These long thick roots are not necessary for feeding the tree but without them the tree would not be able to withstand the onslaughts of nature. When a bonsai tree is potted up, the function of the taproot is taken over by wire or raffia that is used to tie the trees firmly into position. This means that all taproots can be totally eliminated, leaving more room in the pot for the fine feeding roots to grow.

Even where loam is rich and deep, the roots of mature trees show on the surface of the ground to some extent, buttressing the tree

against the elements. As they age, these roots resemble branches, become more rigid and grow a bark-like exterior, but they have a different internal structure from branches, as they serve a different purpose. The surface roots are a significant visual sign of the maturity of the tree and can enhance its appearance of power. This is a very important aspect of bonsai design. A bonsai master will choose a tree to work on by the line of its trunk and the flare of its roots, knowing that all other defects except these can be corrected. Branches can be wired to give them a more aged appearance but wiring roots can cause severe damage.

Soil erosion also causes roots to be exposed and many walkers have tripped over tree roots while walking along woodland paths. In unconfined spaces, roots may find their way around obstacles in their search for water but, where

space is confined, they will flow over whatever is in their way, even if it is a large rock or a building.

When trees and plants colonize a mountain top or rocky outcrop they have to contend with having virtually no soil, restricted moisture and very little fertilizer. The growth pattern here is very different from the general pattern of 'root over rock', where the rock has simply been in the way of the root development. In mountainous regions, roots have to force their way between the rocks or into cracks in the rock to get a hold. The tree is often then left clinging precariously to the rockface, with scant resources, taking decades to develop. Several different species of tree will often colonize one rockface but all the trees tend to be short and stocky with a large part of the tree cascading downwards.

TOP LEFT: The roots of this hawthorn (Crataegus) are exposed and ready to trip up an unwary walker

TOP RIGHT: Roots can even swallow buildings – the roots of huge trees have completely enclosed part of the 1,000-year-old Tah Prom Temple at Angkor in Cambodia

LOWER LEFT: Rock planting – maple, White Pine, juniper and spruce all cling to this piece of Zimbabwean rock

Natural rock planting, Krabi, Thailand: this coastal rock has been colonized by trees and plants and acts as an ideal example for a rock planting

The flowers of some trees are insignificant while others are flamboyant: hibiscus flower (TOP LEFT); rhododendron flower (LOWER LEFT); pine flowers (TOP RIGHT); and tiny juniper flowerbuds (LOWER RIGHT)

Reproduction

The vast majority of trees bear flowers. Often the flowers are small and insignificant, like those on junipers, but on others, such as the hibiscus and the rhododendron, the flowers can be magnificent. The common hawthorn, laburnum and forsythia also look wonderful in the spring. The purpose of these flowers is purely to aid fertilization of the embryonic seeds by which the tree will reproduce itself. Some trees throw out runners, or have lower branches that touch ground and root, but overwhelmingly it is seed germination that produces new trees.

The flowers of common garden trees can also be spectacular: hawthorn (LEFT); and laburnum (RIGHT)

Seeds are dispersed in different ways: hawthorn (TOP LEFT); beech (TOP MIDDLE); (TOP RIGHT); pine sycamore (LOWER LEFT); and laburnum (LOWER RIGHT)

Despite what may be written on the packets of over-priced seeds in some garden centres there is no such thing as 'bonsai tree seeds'. Bonsai trees are developed from ordinary trees, such as those that are seen in the countryside; they are not a separate species. Seeds of native trees are easily collected and just as easily sown. That is the easy bit – getting them to germinate is the problem. A gift set containing a pot, compost, seeds and instructions may be prettily packaged, but it will seldom be satisfactory. In fact, tree seeds deteriorate rapidly, and should be sown fresh and stored only under very specialized conditions.

Tree seeds are most viable when they are ripe and fresh, so start looking for them in your local park or woodland areas as soon as autumn begins. For germination, seeds of different trees need to be treated in different ways; detailed instructions on the propagation of individual tree species can be found in most good gardening encyclopaedias. (For general instructions on growing from seed, *see* Chapter 4.) Don't be over-optimistic about germinating

Bryce Canyon, USA: deadwood on trees can have a very dramatic visual effect

TOP RIGHT: Things are not always as they seem – this tall, lightning-stricken pine is really a garden-centre juniper that has been in training for one year

MIDDLE AND LOWER RIGHT: Natural pruning causes denser twigging. The winter skeleton shows the tree's deadwood and naturally pruned area: the mid-branches of the left-hand side of the tree show that twigging is more dense in areas that have been naturally cut back

LEFT: Oak in Blickling Park, England: the broken branches and hollowed trunk of this old oak reflect the resilience of the spirit of the tree

seeds from the exotic trees you see abroad. The seeds of some tropical trees need to pass through the gut of a bird or an animal before germination takes place, while others need to be baked in the heat of a fire or caught in a winter freeze before they will consider sending out shoots.

Trees and shrubs such as rowan, cotoneaster, hawthorn, pyracantha, and many others, have seeds that are covered in fleshy fruit. This is usually cleaned away in the digestion systems of birds. For home germination, clean this fleshy covering away manually before the seeds are sown, otherwise the seeds may rot. Oak, beech, hazel and other nut trees produce seeds with a hard covering sheath that are usually dispersed by animals. Sycamore and the other maples have winged seeds that are dispersed by the wind. Laburnum, broom and gorse-type shrubs have seeds that are contained in a bean-like pod, which gives an audible 'crack' when it opens, propelling the seeds away from the parent plant. Pines, larches, spruces, cedars and all other coniferous trees and shrubs, by definition, produce cones of some kind. The cone is just a casing; cones that are wide open have already shed the seeds that were inside it.

Natural Pruning

Trees are naturally 'pruned' through the effects of age and weather. Both deciduous and coniferous trees are often seen with deadwood and the jagged edges of branches that have been torn off by the weight of snow or the strength of the wind. Deadwood looks dramatic on coniferous trees that have been struck by lightening, and old deciduous trees with hollow trunks also reflect the spirit of the tree in an awe-inspiring way. Those ancient hardwoods that remain have survived because of their defects – the flaws that caused those hollow trunks. Had they been perfect, they would have been chopped down and used for beams in church roofs or for shipbuilding.

Traditionally, deadwood is only artificially created in coniferous bonsai; any dead branches on deciduous bonsai are removed by pruning.

Natural pruning causes back-budding and increased twigging on branches that have been broken but have areas that are still living. Branches that remain elongated and unpruned have growth that is thinner and more widespread. Pruning with tools has the same result. Shortening branches and twigs causes extra buds to appear and the branch to become more densely twigged and leafed, making the trunk look thicker and the tree

As a tree ages, the ratio between its height and the thickness of its trunk changes: young pine trees (TOP) have an upward surge, a mature churchyard cedar (MIDDLE) bears the weight of its age and this ancient oak (LOWER) is broken but tenaciously clinging to life

These trees are all of different shapes and sizes but each will fit into the shape of an asymmetrical triangle

look older. Where pruning is insufficient to create the overall illusion of age, wiring can be employed to encourage the tree to adopt a particular shape.

Size, Shape and Perspective

The shape of a tree is dictated by its evolution and by its needs. Most coniferous trees from higher ground are tall and slender, with specialized foliage and restricted root growth. Those from lower ground are more dense, with broad leaves and wide-spreading roots.

As a tree ages, the ratio of its height to the width of its trunk changes. Young trees are a bit like teenagers; they have an upward surge of growth that makes them tall and gangly, with spindly trunks and branches. Mature trees have that middle-aged look of a heavier midriff and stronger branches that bear the signs of the life they have lived, and the trials and tribulations they have survived. Ancient trees have the pensioner look of gnarled bent beauty, but with broken bits that no longer work properly.

No living thing is truly symmetrical. Generally, natural trees fit into the shape of a triangle that has sides of different lengths. Even if the tree is growing very straight and tall, it is unlikely that the force of the tree will be in an upward direction only. The tree will also have

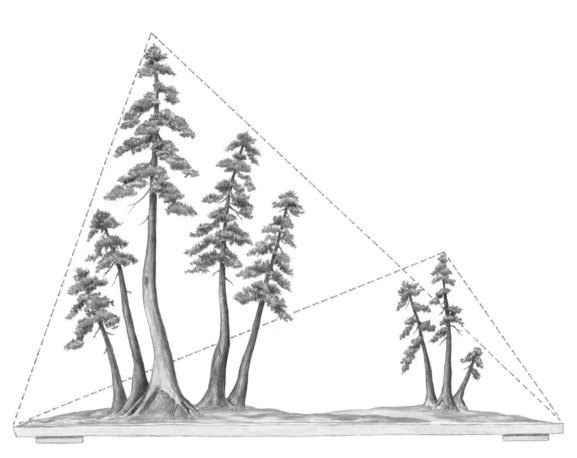

The triangular effect is extremely noticeable where trees have grown in groups or alongside trees of other species. The prevailing winds have much to do with the shape of the group but natural growth plays a bigger part. The trees in the middle of the group have to struggle for light and therefore grow taller than those on the outside of the group where light is more easily found. Also, according to the group's position in relation to the sun, one side will receive more light; the side that is lacking in light will grow taller than the other. This effect is the same, regardless of the size of the trees, and is a significant factor in the creation of bonsai group plantings and of landscapes, which are made up of several triangular-shaped areas within one tray.

Although in nature trees grow where they germinate, and in numbers according to what the land can sustain, the space available in a tray must be put to the best use. One practice, now part of bonsai tradition, plants trees in uneven groups to give an illusion of perspective. This is not, as many suppose, entirely due to the oriental love of odd numbers. In fact, there is a scientific basis for it, recognized by Japanese gardeners centuries ago. When the eye detects a

visual 'movement', causing one side to be visually stronger than the other. This triangular effect is very important in terms of bonsai, if the tree is to look 'right'. The relationship between the tree and its pot is accentuated as the tree's visual force is counterbalanced by its container.

'Baine's Baobabs', Botswana: the tiny Land Cruiser on the left-hand side of the photo gives scale to these massive baobabs which, despite their size and unusual shapes, still fit within an asymmetrical triangle

group with an even number of items the brain divides the groups into smaller more manageable groups. With an uneven number it is not able to do this and so the group has the illusion of being much bigger than it is. Generally, trees are planted as singletons or as pairs, but groups are created by planting three, five, seven or nine trees together. More than nine trees are seen simply as a large group and the brain does not attempt to split them up.

Bonsai is about illusion, and an impression of distance can be created by having large trees at the front of the pot and smaller trees towards the back. In reality, the spacing between the two groups is just inches, but the effect is that the eye tricks the brain into believing that the tallest

trees in each group are the same size, and that the two groups are miles apart.

'Baine's Baobabs' is an example of size and illusion in trees. This group of baobabs in Botswana was painted by the artist Baine in the middle of the nineteenth century. Their age is unknown but comparative drawings and photographs have shown that there has been very little perceptible change in their growth for more than a century. Legend has it that the baobab was so beautiful it thought it could outshine its god; as a punishment, the god turned the tree upside down, burying its head in the sand and leaving its roots in the air, which accounts for the tree's odd appearance. The scale of these trees is put into perspective only by the

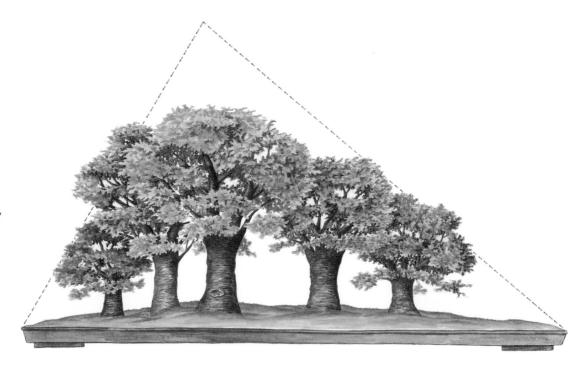

The grandeur of Baine's Baobabs could be re-created on a tray within its natural asymmetrical shape

In order to look natural, this chumono juniper fits within the shape of an asymmetrical triangle

familiar Land Cruiser vehicle in the left-hand corner of the photograph. The incorporation of trees or items of which the size is assumed can give perspective to the whole group and is an illusionary tool that can be put to great use in the design of bonsai landscapes.

Another trick of perspective is the vanishing point. Illusions of size and distance, especially within groups or landscapes, can be created in very small areas with the inclusion of a pathway that starts wide and vanishes into the 'distance', which is in fact only the depth of the pot. The photograph of the ancient pathway through beech woods illustrates this point. Although the pathway appears to go on for miles, in reality it is only a couple of hundred yards long. The eye assumes that the pathway is on flat ground when it actually goes up a fairly steep hill. The same perspective illusion can be created within inches by careful placing of trees and mounds of compost.

ABOVE: Perspective can be gained by adding small plants that masquerade as bushes: this shohin juniper is only approximately 12in (30cm) high, but with the inclusion of a small heather to act as a bush the lonely lakeside scene is complete

LOWER RIGHT: The sacred meets the secular! This tree, in Thailand, is over 6ft (1.5m) but could easily be thought as very small. Perspective is gained through seeing the bicycle and seat, the size of which can be assumed

LOWER LEFT: Ancient pathway through beech woods: this pathway appears to be miles long as it vanishes into the distance but actually covers only a couple of hundred yards

3 Bonsai Sizes and Styles

General Principles

Bonsai owes its name to Japan, and the most commonly found styles of bonsai are also of Japanese origin, although each style takes its lead from nature, depicting trees that have been shaped by different growing environments. The numerous styles, and their variations, are represented by simple descriptive names – such as 'windswept', 'root-over-rock' and 'exposed root' – which give an overall picture of the tree. All the styles have been reclassified many times, to achieve agreement relating to the specific attributes that a tree should have in order to fit into any particular style category.

Over centuries, Japanese masters formed rules to guide others on the 'best practice' for developing these styles, and the variations on them. Although these rules are only guidelines, they are excellent, and recognized as resulting in the most pleasing visual balance to the tree. Like all rules, they are seldom followed rigidly, except by those who wish to train their trees to competition level, but their value should not be underestimated.

No traveller would attempt to find their way around a new town without a guidebook telling them what to see, as well as what to avoid; only with more information could the traveller afford to look for shortcuts or take risks. The same is true of finding a way around a tree. For a newcomer to the art of bonsai, guidelines on how to tackle a tree are as invaluable as a map is to a tourist. With experience, it is possible to move away from the guidelines and develop trees that have a personal touch. In the meantime, however, the guidelines can be of great comfort to novices when they have to decide which branches to prune and which to retain, in order to achieve a particular style.

A collection of bonsai trees, showing the variation in sizes: large Japanese Black Pine, mame Japanese White Pine, miniature azalea, shohin Japanese White Pine

Bonsai Sizes

Traditionally, there are several named sizes of tree, with around thirty to forty variations in style. Within that wide framework every tree is as individual as an original oil painting; not all of them are masterpieces, but all of them are different.

Whatever the size or style of tree chosen, at some time it will need pruning, or wiring and re-potting, if it is to maintain its shape and vigour. For instructions on all of these processes, *see* later chapters.

The groups encompassing bonsai trees of different sizes are specifically named. The smallest are the tiny *keshitsubu* specimens, which are planted in thimble-sized pots that are small enough to balance on the end of a finger. The next size up are the *mame* trees, which, at up to

Very small trees require very frequent watering, and large trees can be difficult for one person to move about and re-pot. The majority of trees held by amateurs are therefore in the medium chumono range, as these are easier to manage; most of the trees shown in this book fit into this category.

Enthusiasts frequently have collections that encompass all sizes and styles but some growers choose to concentrate entirely on mame trees, as these offer a huge challenge. The lifespan of mame trees is usually measured in decades rather than centuries, but they often have an appeal that the more powerful big trees may lack. Small may be beautiful but it is not necessarily easy to achieve.

As bonsai is about illusion, the actual age of the tree is largely immaterial but, whatever their size, all trees should demonstrate all the primary attributes of an aged tree.

Bonsai Styles

Basic Guidelines

There are several 'rules' that relate to bonsai trees in general, regardless of size or style. The first of these is that the tree should have a front and a back. A tree in its natural environment is

6in (15cm) high, including the pot, are small enough to sit in the palm of the hand. *Shohin* trees can be up to 15in (37.5cm) high; *chumono* are medium-sized trees up to 30in (75cm); anything taller than that is a large *omono* tree. 'Large', therefore, covers all trees that are between 2.5ft (75cm) and 10ft (300cm) high, including the pot.

Almost any species of tree can be maintained at any size, but the leaf size of some species obviously limits their suitability for mame.

Two views of a cascade juniper – which is the front and which is the back? It is a well-trained tree, which looks good from all angles, but one 'front' gives a more dramatic outline than the other. The decision over which outline is 'best' lies with its owner

viewed from all angles, but there will always be a viewpoint from which it looks best. In bonsai terms, this would determine the 'front' of the tree. There can be differences of opinion over which is the best aspect of the tree and, over its lifetime, as a tree develops, its 'front' may change several times. Within basic constraints, it is the eye of the owner that the tree has to please, and it is the owner therefore who makes the final decision over the viewing angle. In practice, the front is usually determined by the angle from which most of the tree's faults remain hidden.

Those who have seen bonsai trees only in photographs may have problems of perspective, not only of size but also of depth. Two-dimensional photographs tend to encourage beginners to develop trees with side branches only. Because the front of the tree is clear of branches, beginners mistakenly clear the back of the trunk of branches as well. Study a number of trees from all angles in order to understand the overall visual balance of the tree and to appreciate the importance of rear branches, which add to its depth.

When viewed from the front, the trunk of the tree should be clearly visible and branches should radiate from it in a loose spiral, starting

about one-third of the way up the trunk. No branches should point directly at the viewer and there should be no branches that are directly in line with each other, forming a 'T'. The trunk should taper in a pleasing manner and roots should radiate from its base in an even flare. A finished tree should lean slightly towards the viewer, gently 'bowing its head' as an invitation to come and admire it. Its branches should be downward-sloping and outstretched, as though holding a skirt in a curtsy, acknowledging the viewer's admiration.

Few trees in the wild match up to these criteria and it is a tall order for young bonsai trees to match. Unless you are buying a finished tree, you will need patience and time in order to encourage a tree to fit into any desired shape. This is where the rules come into play. They will help you take the appropriate steps to achieve the style for which you are aiming.

Selecting a Style

Before selecting a style for a tree, it is vital to consider its natural growing habits. Remember that the tree is a living thing and should be encouraged to grow in a particular style, not forced into it. If a tree is unhappy with its treatment and growing conditions, it will protest; if it is seriously mistreated, it will die.

A knowledge of the habit of a tree is invaluable in knowing how to treat the tree during styling. You may be impressed by professional demonstrations, but you should not try to replicate all the design treatments you see. These demonstrations are largely done for entertainment, and many trees styled in this quick-fix way do not live long.

Years ago, at a bonsai workshop, horticultural skills bowed to design skills, when two tall graceful trees were turned into short dramatic masterpieces. The trees were about twenty years old and supported low branches that had given them thick trunks with good bases and character. Both trunks were severed immediately above the first branch and the trunks were nipped away to give the required taper. The single branch of each tree was wired to the last twig and bent into a shape that was visually wonderful. Both trees were resplendent in their new form for a whole week, then rapidly died. The treatment of the trees was too harsh; styling should have taken place over years, not hours.

Styles for Single Trees

There are five basic styles suitable for single trees, each relating to the angle of its trunk:

1   Formal upright: *Chokkan*
2   Informal upright: *Moyogi*
3   Slanting: *Shakan*
4   Semi-cascade: *Han-Kengai*
5   Cascade: *Kengai*

There are thirty or more variations on the five basic styles, with the same trunk forms, but with sufficiently different branch or root placement to warrant style categories of their own. Sometimes a tree will have features from several styles, making it difficult to place in any particular category. Enthusiasts sometimes spend many an hour trying to decide which competition category to enter. However, if the tree is pleasing to the eye and looks convincing as a tree, then its style is not a matter for concern.

Other single tree styles include the following:

6   Broom: *Hokidachi*
7   Literati: *Bunjingi*
8   Windswept: *Fukinagashi*
9   Exposed root: *Ne Agari*

Unusual forms include the following:

10   Driftwood: *Sharamiki*
11–13   Hollow trunk (*Sabakan*), knobbly trunk (*Kobukan*) and spiral trunk (*Nejikan*)

Additional styles can incorporate rocks and figures, as follows:

14   Root-over-rock: *Sekijoju*
15   Root-on-rock: *Ishitsuki*

Styles for Single Trees with Several Trunks

Single trees can also have several trunks giving the impression that there are a number of trees in the planting:

16   Twin and triple trunks: *Sokan and Tosho*
17   Root-connected clump: *Kabudachi*
18   Raft and sinuous: *Ikadabuki and Netsunagari*

Group Plantings and Landscapes

Group plantings and landscapes are limited only by the size of the container.

19   Group planting: *Yose-ue*
20   Landscapes: *Saikei and Bonkei*

There are further variations on the above styles but the differences are relatively minor and of more interest to the professional than to the amateur.

The Basic Styles

Formal Upright – Chokkan

A formal upright is exactly as its name suggests. It stands grand and straight like a natural tree that has not suffered any deprivation, crowding or harsh weather conditions. The specimen sequoias that grace the gardens of stately homes are a good example of the formal upright style. It is not an easy style to reproduce as it calls for a completely straight trunk and evenly spaced branches. Material with these attributes is not always easy to find and a beginner should start with a less formal, more forgiving style of tree.

The tree should have a distinct taper of trunk from base to apex and, although it should still fit into the usual asymmetrical triangular shape, this will be less obvious than in some other styles. Having a completely upright trunk, the apex of the tree should sit directly above its base. Conifers such as larch, pine and spruce are better suited to this style than deciduous trees, which have a more informal habit. To look 'right' the formal upright bonsai should be taller than it is wide, like a sequoia, or wider than it is tall, like an ancient cedar. It should never sit in its pot in a nondescript square.

After the decision about which is the tree's front, the placement of the branches is very important in a formal upright. The lowest of the branches should also be the thickest and the most densely twigged and foliated. It is this branch that determines the size, slant and shape of all the other branches. This first branch should come off the trunk at about one-third of the way up; it can point either to the left or to the right, but should be pointing slightly

Formal upright pine and parkland sequoia: formal upright trees should be either wider than they are tall, like the bonsai pine tree (LEFT), or taller than they are wide, like the parkland sequoia (RIGHT)

forwards, towards one of the front 'corners' of the pot. Once the lowest branch has been located, the other branches can be placed in relation to it. The second branch should be a smaller, thinner version of the first branch and should point to the opposite front 'corner' of the pot.

It is at this point that the rear of the tree often gets neglected. The third branch should be at the rear of the tree, to give it visual depth and perspective. All the other branches should be placed in the same way, ensuring that they get

thinner and shorter towards the apex of the tree.

In bonsai form, a formal upright tree should be planted in a pot that is equally formal, preferably in a simple shallow rectangular, square or round shape. Bright colours and elaborate pots should be avoided.

Informal Upright – Moyogi

The shape of the informal upright is the one most commonly seen in nature. Therefore it suits most bonsai species, both of coniferous and deciduous trees. The informal upright resembles a tree that has had some form of deprivation, not too harsh, but enough to provide character to its shape. Wind, lack of light and competition from other trees might well have caused the trunk of this type of tree to shift in direction from time to time, to increase its chances of survival. The most beautiful of the bonsai maples are usually in this style. The look of the tree will change with the seasons. Many deciduous trees, such as beech, are at their best in the winter months when their leaves have fallen and their branches are fully revealed.

The same basic rules that apply to the formal upright also apply to the informal upright,

Formal upright chumono Trident Maple: this tree has a thick trunk and promising root structure. It will eventually be planted in a shallow rectangular pot

Formal upright omono larch (Larix): this tree is complete with cones. Leaving fruits or seed forms on a tree causes it stress and the cones on this tree will be removed shortly, to allow the tree to recover

except that the trunk of the informal upright has one or more curves, which can veer either very gently or dramatically in one direction or another, but never towards the viewer. As the tree is an upright its apex must still remain over its base but the asymmetrical shape will be more pronounced than in the formal upright style.

Informal upright chumono Japanese Maple deshojo

The informal upright is a good starting point for the beginner. As the 'rules' are much less rigid than those relating to formal trees, a convincing tree can be developed over a reasonably short space of time, producing a feeling of achievement. Starting with raw material that has a decent trunk and root flare, a bonsai of this style can be achieved with about four years of selective pruning and careful wiring.

Mame-sized informal upright Chinese Elm with exquisite twigging (LEFT), and a tiny cotoneaster complete with berries (RIGHT); the cotoneaster will be moved into a much smaller container when it is next re-potted

39

LEFT: Shohin-sized informal upright Satsuki azalea

RIGHT: Chumono-sized slanting-style beech

Chumono-sized informal upright Japanese Maple in round glazed pot

The informal upright style lends itself to a wide range of pots of a size and depth that will suit the species of tree. Flowering and fruiting trees can be planted in pots that complement their colours but other species of tree should be planted in muted pots that blend in with the tree.

Slanting Style and its Windswept Style Variant – Shakan and Fukinagashi

A slanting style tree emulates one that has been subjected to strong winds that have caused it to partially lose its footings and lean into the wind. Alternatively, it could mimic one that has been deprived of light, which has caused it to

move from its upright position in search of the sun. The slant of the tree is noticeable but not extreme, with an angle usually of less than 45 degrees. If the trunk slants at a much greater angle, it becomes more of a semi-cascade than a slanting style tree.

The trunk can lean to the left or to the right but not forward and should be fairly straight without curves. The roots of the tree should appear to anchor it firmly to the ground, looking particularly strong 'upwind' of its slant.

The tree will not have suffered hardship to the extent that it has been stripped of branches on one side. Neither will it (unlike a windswept tree) have been caused to have all its branches pointing into the prevailing wind. The branches will be fairly well balanced and distributed but, because of the slant, the apex of the tree will no longer be over its base.

A windswept style represents a tree that has suffered far greater hardships than a slanting one. Its lean can be quite severe and the force of the wind will have caused all of its branches to point in the same direction. The direction of the branches is not necessarily the same as that of the trunk – the tree will often lean one way and the branches another – but all the branches will point the same way. Windswept trees are often very dramatic and can incorporate a lot of deadwood. Pines, junipers and larches lend themselves particularly well to these styles.

Before starting to prune away branches on raw material, make a pencil sketch of the tree showing the basic placement of its branches. Erase the branches that you want to remove and decide on the shape and direction in which the remaining branches are to be wired. This way,

you will have a good idea of the outcome before you start. To achieve a windswept style, it may be necessary to wire all of the tree's branches; a beginner can do this in stages as they gain experience and confidence.

Slanting and windswept trees are suitable for most shallow pots, but they look best on rock slabs and artificial rocks. Ceramic shells are also good at displaying the tree's ruggedness. As the weight of the tree is not centralized it will need to be carefully wired on to a slab or into a pot to stop it falling over.

Cascade and Semi-Cascade – Kengai and Han-Kengai

In the wild a cascade tree would be found clinging to a mountainside. Its root development would be severely restricted and, as it would be impossible for the tree to grow in an upright position, the sheer weight of its branches would have caused them to 'cascade' down the mountainside. The branches of semi-cascades move more towards the horizontal than the vertical; they may be found on mountainsides, but they are more usually found leaning over the water beside a lake or a river.

A formal cascade style has an apex resembling a separate small upright tree (*see* the collected yew, page 42). Inspection of a tree such as this will show that it is the lowest of its branches that forms the cascade. The branch will have thickened and elongated to such an extent that it now resembles the trunk itself. In an informal cascade and in a semi-cascade, the cascade is formed from the actual trunk of the tree not its branches.

If a naturally cascading tree is not found, material can be trained into this style by gradually wiring the trunk of a young flexible tree

or allowing the lowest branch of a more mature tree to elongate, and wiring or weighting it downwards. As trees have a natural habit of growing upwards, laying the tree on its side can encourage the tree to grow towards the light, which will ultimately affect the angle of its trunk.

In bonsai form, a cascade tree will be in a tall pot, usually of a square or hexagonal shape and preferably secured to a bench, as the cascade may descend well below the bottom of the pot. Semi-cascade trees have a lean in excess of 45 degrees and may descend to below the rim of the pot but they do not descend as low as cascade trees. The pots of semi-cascade trees are wider and not so tall as those of cascade trees but are usually deeper than those used for windswept style trees. Cascade trees can also be planted on tall rocks or incorporated with trees of other styles on rock plantings.

LEFT: Slanting style shohin English Elm in a ceramic shell

RIGHT: Windswept chumono San Jose Juniper on an artificial slab, in the process of being pruned

BELOW: Semi-cascade mame cotoneaster in tall square glazed pot

LEFT: *Informal cascade shohin Zelkova: an informal cascade does not have an apex*

RIGHT: *Broom style Chinese Elm: Chinese Elm and Zelkova are ideal for broom style, as they grow quickly and twig freely*

Formal cascade chumono collected yew (Taxus baccata): this tree, which has a defined apex and a long cascade, has only been in training for eighteen months since being collected from a chalk pit

the winter silhouette of a broom style tree has unmatchable grace and beauty.

The trunk of a broom style tree is always straight and upright. Its branches, through selective pruning, continuously divide until over the years until a ball of twigging is formed. Because of their readiness to twig, Chinese Elms, *Zelkova*, beech, hornbeam and stewartia are the favourite species for growing in this style. Coarse-branched trees and conifers are not suitable to be grown in a broom fashion.

To start the training of a broom style tree choose one that already has a straight thick trunk; this might involve finding a tree of considerable height. Saw the trunk off at a level where you want the first branches to sprout. Leaving this will result in an ugly untapered stump at the top of the trunk; to alleviate this, cut a deep notch in the top of the trunk and

Style Variations

Broom Style – Hokidachi

This style of tree derives its name from a Japanese sweeping brush or broom, and most closely resembles the lollipop trees often drawn by children. Many trees that start their bonsai training in a broom style are eventually radically restyled, as the broom shape is not an easy one to develop. However, if it can be achieved,

The winter silhouette of a natural broom-style parkland tree

TOP LEFT AND BOTTOM LEFT: Broom style chumono trees in a Japanese bonsai centre. The red 'flowers' on top of the compost are insecticide

TOP RIGHT AND LOWER RIGHT: Literati style shohin junipers

bind the two sides together. The two parts may meld and new branches form all around the top. Allow these branches to extend until they have thickened and then prune them all back as evenly as growth will permit. The pruning process has to be repeated continuously until the broom is complete.

Broom style trees are always grown in very shallow pots, of a wide range of shapes.

Literati Style – Bunjingi

The gaunt lonely Scot's Pine of the seashore or mountainside demonstrates this style naturally. The trunk is long and slender, either straight or with numerous bends, but there are no side branches and only a small amount of foliage on the apex. The bends can be gentle or tortuous as the tree wends its way upwards towards the light, having shed its lower branches through many years of hardship. Coniferous species are best suited to this style although flowering trees such as hawthorn and cotoneaster can also be effective.

It is a style in which few of the 'rules' of bonsai apply and is more in tradition with the original Chinese philosophy of allowing the spirit of the tree to follow its own path. The name is thought to have originated in reference to the scholars and artists (literati) who practised the calligraphic arts and drew the magnificent minimalist ink-wash paintings of the Sung Dynasty. As there are few rules, it is a style on which to put an individual stamp, following what the tree's designer feels the tree should do rather than what tradition dictates that it should do.

The main mistake made with the literati design is to have too much foliage in relation to the tree's trunk. The thin trunk will only look like a mature one if everything else is in balance and that includes the foliage. If there is excessive foliage, the tree will look like a weedy sapling instead of an aged tree.

43

Exposed Root Style – Ne Agari

Trees that grow around riverbanks, and other areas that are prone to erosion, often have their roots gradually exposed until a whole network of roots is revealed. Many innocent walkers have had their ankles wrenched by wayward tree roots. Tropical trees also often have exposed roots, but for a different reason; these are aerial roots that have grown *down* from the branches to gather extra moisture and are not roots that would be normally have been underground.

With careful treatment and slow exposure of the roots most tree species can be styled in this manner. Train the tree by planting it in a tall plastic pot, which can be intermittently cut away, making the pot shorter and shorter, very gradually exposing the tree's roots to the air. The roots soon turn dark in colour and develop a bark-like exterior coating. Alternatively, raise the tree slightly, exposing a little more root, each time it is re-potted until the desired amount of root is showing.

The intricate roots of this twin-trunk chumono hornbeam have been carefully exposed

Exposed-root omono Satsuki azalea: trees can be planted in tall pots and the upper roots exposed as the lower roots extend until the above effect is achieved

Unusual Styles for Single Trees

Driftwood Style – Sharamiki

Driftwood style trees take their name from the weathered, bleached white lumps of wood and roots that are seen washed up on seashores. They have large areas of deadwood, often elaborately carved, leaving the observer wondering how the tree has survived with so little remaining living tissue. Junipers and yews respond well to this treatment but it can also be applied with care to deciduous trees, although this is not so commonly done. In trees that have grown in particularly harsh environments, like the one in Bryce Canyon (*see* page 27), this deadwood effect would have occurred naturally, but in most bonsai trees the look has to be artificially induced with the aid of scalpels and power tools. Deadwood areas on branches are called *jins* and strips of deadwood on trunks are called *sharis*. For instructions on how to create and create *jins* and *sharis*, *see* Chapter 11 (page 110).

The front of the tree is often completely stripped of bark except for a small ribbon of live wood through which nutrients can flow. The rear of the tree, which the viewer will not see, is left intact except for those areas where the carving goes all the way through the trunk.

Applying a lime sulphur solution creates the bleached white appearance of driftwood. In addition to the bleaching effect, the lime sulphur will help to preserve the wood and delay its ultimate decay. The treatment will need to be repeated on an annual basis if the deadwood is to stay white as moulds attack the deadwood, leaving it green or black. Colouring agents can be added to the lime sulphur if the whiteness is considered to be too harsh.

LEFT: Elaborately carved driftwood style chumono lilac (Syringa) created from a collected stump

RIGHT: Omono Needle Juniper (Juniperus rigida) in a driftwood style: this tree has been wrapped around the root of an old pine tree. It is only fifteen years old, but the effect is to create an image of an ancient tree that has suffered many hardships

Dieback of branches above areas of trunk treated in this way is unavoidable and often the tree will die after being given extensive driftwood styling. Carefully protect the treated tree from sunlight or frost. Alternatively, create a driftwood effect using a young tree wrapped around an old piece of wood. Old roots are good for this purpose as they are hard and have the necessary visual characteristics. Eventually, the two separate items meld together as a whole, creating a remarkable deadwood effect.

If the old driftwood style piece of wood does not stand straight a footing will need to be attached to give it stability. The young tree will need to be fixed to the driftwood in some way to hold it firmly in position so that it looks as though it is a strip of living wood on an ancient tree. The usual advice is to cut a spiral channel into the old wood, and to glue the slim trunk into it. However, if the new tree is healthy (and it should be), it will grow and quickly force its way out of the channel. Tie, or wire the tree into place. As it ages and hardens it will adopt its new position.

The juniper pictured above right was created in this way. It is only fifteen years old but already has the look of an ancient tree that has survived countless hardships and retained its regal state against all the odds. This is an excellent example of using basic techniques to create an illusion; in fact, no area of the living tree has been stripped of bark.

Driftwood style trees need pots of the heavy rugged type, in dark or muted colours that will complement their power and give balance to their shape.

Hollow Trunk, Twisted Trunk and Knobbly Trunk Styles

Just as some trees are developed purely for their spring flowers, which more than compensates for later problems with their leaves and growth patterns, some trees are grown for the visual splendours of their trunk.

Hollow trunk, twisted trunk and knobbly trunk styles fall into this category. They are not common as they require unusual material to start off with. They are not always classically

Collected English Elm: a hollow trunk clump developed from a stump. This wonderful tree tells its own story

LEFT: *Collected stump of chumono forsythia in a deep unglazed pot: in addition to the pleasure of its flowers, the trunk of this collected garden shrub is visually extremely powerful*

RIGHT: *Chumono Cork-Bark Elm, enhanced by its knobbly bark*

beautiful trees that obey the rules of design but they have character, power and interest. For hollow trunks, unless suitable material can be collected from the wild (*see* the elm on page 45), it is necessary to have a really heavy stump that will lend itself to carving. The Trident Maple pictured on page 74, which was a plain stump two years ago, has been hollowed out with power tools. It is still undergoing treatment but already resembles an aged oak. Eventually, this tree will have most of its heartwood removed and its upper branches styled and extended.

Twisted trunk trees in nature may have grown around things or been constricted in some way;

Omono Japanese Black Pine with the effect of a twisted trunk

a young tree that has been strangled by honeysuckle, for example, takes on a highly spiral form. Old junipers sometimes hang on to life through a spiral of living tissue that winds its way around a largely dead trunk. Sometimes, an illusion of this spiral effect can be produced, by creating deadwood on the front part of the trunk, which only looks as though it spirals around the tree. A spiralling effect can also be created by applying heavy wiring to the trunk in order to distort it. The Japanese Black Pine pictured lower left has been grown for its trunk, which has the effect of twisting several times before the first branch appears.

Knobbly trunks are the result of extensive scarring, which in some cases can lead to interest rather than to ugliness. If at any time a tree has suffered extensive root damage, which may have caused part of the tree to die back or chunks of bark to fall off, there will also be extensive damage to the trunk. Some trees, such as the Cork-Bark Elm, have very distinctive bark that is naturally knobbly.

Styles Using Rocks

Root-over-Rock – Sekijoju

In rocky terrain the roots of a tree will flow over almost anything, in a constant search for moisture and nutrients. These trees do not only grow on high ground; rocky outcrops are found in

Root-on-Rock – Ishitsuki

low-level woodlands as well as on mountain slopes. Rocky areas in lowland woods produce beeches, birches, oaks and flowering trees that have tenaciously spread their roots over everything in their path. Both coniferous and deciduous trees, particularly maples, look excellent in this form.

With a root-over-rock style the roots flow over the rock and then into the pot in which the rock stands. With training, the roots of the tree will grip the rock firmly so that there is no movement of the tree and the tree and the rock become inseparable. For details on creating root-over-rock style trees, *see* Chapter 13.

The purpose of planting on a rock is to create a scene. In order to be convincing, the rock planting needs to tell a story of some kind and, unless something really dramatic is sought, it is unlikely that a tree would take root on a rock in total isolation. Adding heather to act as bushes, and ferns or small alpine plants to lodge in other crevasses, softens the planting. The rock itself should have height, great character and a good colour, preferably with many fissures into which greenery would lodge.

To give prominence to the rock, the pots used for this style are wide, extremely shallow and kept completely devoid of soil. Sometimes they are filled with water, which will reflect the rock

RIGHT: Root-over-rock group of Japanese White Pines: normally, trees that are grown on rocks rather than over them stand in trays devoid of compost. The roots of this group are able to flow over the rock into the pot

LEFT: Root-over-rock Trident Maple

LEFT: A solitary Blaaus Juniper has been planted on this rock giving the effect of a deserted windswept island

RIGHT: Dramatic scene of a rock-planted juniper group softened with underplanting: to ensure that the foliage within the group is all of the same size and colour, this 'group' has been formed from a single raft style tree

Twin-trunk Japanese Maple: the second trunk of this maple follows the same line as the dominant branch

and the tree or trees on it giving the effect of an island rising from the sea.

For details of planting trees on rocks, and of creating raft plantings similar to that pictured (*see* Chapter 13).

Styles for Single Trees with Several Trunks

Triple-trunk stewartia: this balanced tree has a dominant trunk at the front and shorter, thinner trunks to the rear

Twin-Trunk and Triple-Trunk Styles – Sokan and Tosho

Sometimes, two or three trunks may come up from the same root, giving the impression of several trees planted in close proximity. The effect is very pleasing. However, for a true twin- or triple-trunk effect, the division must take place very near or below soil level. It is seldom possible to utilize low branches in this way, as an unconvincing 'wishbone' effect may be created. However, positioning the tree in such a way that it is seen from a slightly sideways angle can alleviate this effect.

The tree should have one trunk that is larger and more dominant than the other – a father and son pair, with one reflecting the characteristics of the other. They should never be of the same size; then, they would be in competition and a catapult effect would be created. The same applies to three- and five-trunk plantings; the children may surround their parent but they should not compete with it, or with their siblings.

In shaping twin- or triple-trunk trees, the inner part is treated as though it is a single tree.

Most of the inner branches and foliage are removed, leaving the outer branches to be developed in relation to each other.

Clump Style – Kabudashi

When several trunks come up from one root, giving the effect of a group, it is referred to as a clump, or root-connected style. It is still only one tree but the multiple trunks have the effect of a close-knit copse. It is important that the trunks rise at surface level. If the trunks rise from below the surface the effect will be of separate trees rather than one clump.

Ideally, any clump should have a dominant trunk, with several smaller and thinner subsidiary trunks all fitting into the usual asymmetrical triangular shape. When pruning a

LEFT: The trunks of twin-trunk and triple-trunk trees should start at surface level, to eliminate the undesirable wishbone effect (RIGHT)

LEFT: Clump style Japanese Maple: there are seven trunks to this clump, all rising at soil level

RIGHT: The same Japanese Maple clump with seven trunks of differing thickness. The dominant tree is both the thickest and the tallest

clump it should be treated as a group, with the inside reasonably devoid of foliage and the outside pruned as though it were one tree.

Clumps, like groups, should be in shallow pots; oval pots look particularly good.

Whereas most species of tree can be treated in the raft style, few conifers naturally form clumps and many would not create a pleasing whole. Fortunately, several deciduous trees, such as hawthorn, field maple and quince, among others, naturally throw up suckers from their roots and form clumps.

Taking an air layering from an unwanted branch that has a cartwheel of foliage can provide possible material for a clump. Alternatively, if a stump is cut to just above root level, it may form a set of adventitious buds around the trunk, which could later be used to form a clump of trunks. However, this leaves the problem of how to get rid of the ugly stump in the middle of the clump. Where possible, use a clump if one forms naturally, but use a sinuous or raft style if nothing else is available.

The maple pictured above is a naturally formed clump, with seven thick trunks all coming from its single root. The result is both pleasing and convincing. When this clump started its training its trunks were completely devoid of branches; all the branch growth has taken place in the last four years.

Raft and Sinuous Style – Ikadabuki and Netsuragari

In forest and woodland, you will sometimes see living trees that have at some time lost their footings and fallen. The branches of these fallen trees start to grow upwards towards the light like new trees, and roots begin to form where the trunk touches the ground. In past decades, this rooting was deliberately induced in parkland trees, such as the plane, leaving the tree surrounded by arched branches each tipped with a new tree. The effect was of an elderly grandparent surrounded by perfectly cloned grandchildren. When the old tree died, new trees with exactly the same characteristics were ready to take its place. A circular copse would be created, radiating from the parent tree like spokes from a wheel. This technique was also employed for creating density in beech hedges.

For bonsai this method is not used simply for reproduction, but also to create the illusion of a group of trees from the branches of a single tree. When the old trunk is straight and the new trees are intended to run in a straight line it is called a raft. When the old trunk wriggles and bends it is called sinuous. Raft style trees and sinuous style trees can be collected from the wild, like the English Elm pictured (*see* page 50), but rooting can also be established in bonsai trees as in parkland trees. For details on how to prepare a raft style planting *see* Chapter 14.

Collected raft style tree: the branches of this tree have become trunks of new trees; the trunk has rooted, forming a raft from which the new 'trees' grow

Collected raft style English Elm (Ulmus procera)*: when this tree was first collected the 'trunks' of the new trees were simple twigs. They have been developed in relation to each other by selective pruning over ten years*

TOP RIGHT: *In order to be convincing, a group should tell a story. Three-tree planting of larch: the roots of these three trees have intertwined as their trunks form a close group. The angle of the planting is very evocative of a mountain group as they move from upright to semi-cascade*

MIDDLE: *Beech group bonsai does not have to be expensive: this group was put together four years ago from a bundle of bare-rooted hedging plants*

What story does this tell? Large juniper group planted on an artificial slab

Multiple and Group Plantings – *Yose Ue*

Two or more trees of the same species can be combined in a planting to create the impression of anything from a lonely pair of trees to a large forest. With up to nine trees, plantings are thought to be multiple and should always be in odd numbers. With more than nine trees, the planting is classified as a forest group and the exact number of trees becomes largely irrelevant. An exception to this rule is for two trees that act as a father and son pair like twin-trunk trees.

If a group planting is to be convincing, its crown must adopt an asymmetrical triangular shape and the trees must be unevenly spaced, with trunks of varying thickness.

Where two trees are concerned, the trees should not be of the same size, but they should always be of the same species. If the trunk of the smaller tree is half the thickness of that of the larger tree, then it should also be half the height. The proportional relationship between the two trees should remain the same. The larger tree should be planted slightly forward of the smaller tree and on slightly higher ground. When pruning, the group should be treated as though it is one tree, and kept within an asymmetrical shape.

Three is a significant number in oriental arts, representing the triumvirate of heaven, earth and man. When three trees are planted, the largest of the trees should be on the highest ground and, to add perspective to the group, it should also be slightly to the fore of the others. Where more than three trees are involved they are still planted in odd numbers but they may be placed in more than one group. Each group should complement but not mirror the other, and each should contain a different number of trees.

The roots of the three larch trees pictured opposite have intertwined as they have been close planted. The angle of the trunks moves from upright to semi-cascade, all within a triangular shape. Work is still being done to add curve to the trunk of the lower tree but the whole effect is of a powerful mountainside group. The composition tells a story. The story may be different for each observer; one interpretation might be that it is a place that is idyllic for a summer picnic but should be avoided as darkness falls and never visited when there is a full moon.

Multiple plantings and groups should always be in shallow pots. The shape of the pot will depend on the nature of the planting. Maples look good in shallow oval pots whereas large groups of conifers look good on rough stone slabs, which can also be produced artificially.

For further details of group plantings *see* Chapter 14. For instructions on how to make an artificial slab *see* Chapter 15.

Landscapes – Saikei and Bonkei

It may be important for a group to tell a story, but for a landscape planting it is absolutely vital. Landscapes need to be well thought out and planned if they are to create a convincing scene. Often, the constituent parts of landscapes

Mixed tree landscape planting in a 3-ft (90-cm) long gravel tray

are governed by their availability, but how they are put together is entirely within the designer's domain. For dramatic landscapes and wilderness the minimalist approach – the 'less is more' philosophy – is the wisest, but for softer landscapes, almost anything is possible. To the bonsai purist, landscapes are anathema, but they do give amateurs the chance to practise horticultural skills and to let the imagination fly. There are no rules governing landscapes. Common sense should be applied to the overall proportions and shape in a search for a realistic look.

A simple landscape can be made from one tree, a few rocks, some moss and a little sand set in a simple tray. The tree is not necessarily planted over or on the rock; the rocks are there to suggest a rocky or mountainous landscape. While group plantings only ever use one species of tree, landscapes allow different species to be put together effectively. Some landscapes are so large and elaborate that they include small buildings and figurines, as well as caves, mountains and beaches. They are an excellent way of re-creating a favourite place to brighten up a desolate balcony or fill a forlorn window box.

For details on how to create landscapes *see* Chapter 13. Instructions on how to create the landscape pictured above are given in Chapter 15.

Adding rocks turns a simple tree into a whole landscape

4 Buying and Growing Bonsai Material

Mature, Japanese-trained trees can cost tens of thousands of pounds

General Principles

When selecting material for bonsai growing the first thing to be considered is where you will keep it. Native trees have evolved to grow in the countryside, not in centrally heated homes. They will adapt to growing in a pot in your garden but they will not survive conditions indoors for more than a few days. A native tree such as a maple, juniper or pine must be grown outside, and should only be brought inside occasionally for display, if at all. Some species, such as Chinese Elm (*Ulmus*) and Japanese Elm (*Zelkova*), are more tolerant of a dry atmosphere with restricted light, but a tropical tree is the only type to keep permanently inside your home. This limits your choice; in this category, previously styled trees are likely to be the only ones available. Owners with a garden, balcony, window box or access to a flat roof will have a much wider choice.

There are several ways of getting a bonsai tree of your own:

- buy a tree that has already been styled and planted in a bonsai pot;
- find a tree in the wild that has been shaped by nature;
- buy a garden-centre tree and style it yourself;
- air layer the branch of a tree or shrub;
- take cuttings from garden trees and shrubs; or
- grow new trees from collected seed.

The quickest and easiest of these options is obviously to buy a tree that has already been styled, but the most satisfactory is the one that involves styling the tree yourself. There is not only the pride of ownership but also the pride of achievement. Growing new trees by grafting is a specialized task that requires expertise and experience. Grafting to obtain new trees is not recommended until you are proficient in bonsai care, although it can be used to obtain new branches where they are reluctant to grow.

Whether buying a finished tree or growing from seed, the same overall characteristics should be sought. Try to find a robust tree that is not too temperamental and has, or is able to develop, small leaves or needles, a strong trunk and good roots.

Buying a Bonsai Tree

What to Look For

For a first bonsai tree, or for a gift for an inexperienced friend, choose a simple, healthy but inexpensive tree. For novices, distressing tree fatalities are frequent. Maples are often considered to be the prettiest trees, with their magnificent colour, while pines evoke feelings of power and strength, but junipers and the Japanese and Chinese Elms are much more tolerant of inexperience and neglect.

When selecting a tree, a professional bonsai 'artist' will look at the tree's trunk line and root flare (*nebari*), knowing that any faults in the size and placement of the tree's branches and twigs can be corrected by careful pruning, wiring or grafting. If a branch is considered to be in the wrong place, it can be cut off and another branch grafted elsewhere, but little can be done to make radical changes to the placement of the tree's roots or to the main characteristics of its trunk.

When selecting your tree, follow the experts and look carefully at its trunk and its roots. The trunk should have an interesting line to it and should have an even taper, becoming progressively thinner towards the top, with as few visible scars as possible. Old pruning scars that have healed well can add interest to the trunk but large scars on field-grown trees that have been cut down should be hidden at the back. The roots should flare evenly from the trunk, not just on one side, and should show on the surface of the compost. There should be no ugly humps on the surface roots either.

Check to see if the tree is firm in its pot. Look underneath to see if roots are protruding through the drainage holes. Branch faults can often be rectified over the years, as new branches and extra twigging can be encouraged, but the best trees will have evenly spaced branches that do not obscure the trunk line. Inspect the leaves thoroughly to make sure that they have a good colour and that none are dying back without good cause, and that no pests or diseases are lurking anywhere.

Where to Buy

As the popularity of the hobby has increased, the number of different places from which you can buy bonsai trees has grown. They can now be found in specialist bonsai centres, garden centres, DIY stores, supermarkets and even high-profile auction houses such as Sotheby's. Naturally, there is a great diversity in quality and price. Good bonsai trees are unavoidably expensive because their development takes many years and is very labour-intensive. Unless you are buying a tree through a bonsai club, a cheap bonsai is either a good bargain or a poor tree.

Larger garden centres may stock a range of imported trees. These might have become slightly overgrown while they are on show but, as they generally cost somewhere between £10 and £100 and are attractive, they are still good

LEFT: Clamps can be used to rectify minor problems or introduce character to a trunk. Minor trunk faults can be remedied, but avoid buying trees that have major faults or lack any character

RIGHT: Garden centres stock a limited range of small and medium-sized bonsai for between £10 and £100

Bonsai centre, East Anglia, England: bonsai centres stock a range of trees, pots and books

courses giving guidance on the development of specific trees.

Bonsai trade fairs are becoming increasingly popular, with experienced bonsai artists giving demonstrations and offering advice. Trade stands provide a wide range of trees, pots, tools and accessories. Flower shows such as those of the Royal Horticultural Society are good places to view trees and bonsai club members sometimes show and sell trees in local venues. Specialist bonsai car boot sales are a new phenomenon, offering the opportunity to purchase bonsai trees inexpensively. (Bonsai trees also appear at general car boot sales, although the quality tends to be very poor and rooted cuttings are often fobbed off as bonsai trees to the unsuspecting.)

value. Some centres will give a guarantee with the plant as long as care guidelines are followed.

For the best trees it is necessary to visit a specialist bonsai centre. Look in the back of gardening or bonsai magazines or try your local *Yellow Pages*. Bonsai centres stock both native and imported trees ranging in price from tens up to thousands of pounds, and they are good places to visit to see mature trees. Staff will usually give you the benefit of their experience and willingly advise you on the care of a particular tree. Many bonsai centres run workshop

Hopeless Cases?

The Japanese Elm (*Zelkova*) pictured (*see* page 55) is typical of one that might be bought from a supermarket, DIY store or car boot sale. It cost less than £10 but is a poor example and explains why most of the trees that are bought as presents quickly die. The tree had not undergone proper bonsai training – its trunk had merely been cut at a low level and allowed to sprout in all directions. There was an ugly dead

White beech (LEFT) and crab apple (RIGHT): mature trees of this quality can be bought from bonsai nurseries and centres for around £200–500

Not a good tree but salvageable: this 'bonsai' Zelkova has merely been cut back and re-potted. The trunk has no taper and ends abruptly where it was cut. It has thick roots and the centre of the rootball (RIGHT) is almost devoid of compost

lump of wood in the middle of the tree and, although the trunk had a reasonable line, it had no taper. Some long shoots had been cut back by an inexperienced shop assistant but nothing had been done to thin them out.

The species and approximate age of the tree was shown on the label, but although the tree was several years old it had been field-grown and had only been in the pot for a relatively short time. As its roots were still heavy and few fine roots had developed, the tree had been crammed into its pot, leaving very little room for compost. Ordinary potting compost had been used, and had clogged up the roots, encouraging root rot (*see* Chapter 9). Without immediate attention, the tree's long-term chances of survival were slim.

All was not lost, however. Removing heavy growth and excess foliage, and snipping away the ugly lump at the top of the tree to create a taper, made an immediate impact. Cutting back the thick old roots and re-potting the tree in open free-draining compost in a more suitable pot should encourage the development of fine feeder roots. The tree looks bare at the moment but it now has a framework for development and in a short time it will have recovered and be on its way to producing a fine shohin-sized bonsai. All those twigs that have been cut off can be used as cuttings to make more trees. Beginners are usually reluctant to remove more than a minimal amount of growth but sometimes it is necessary to cut a tree back hard to let its natural shape re-emerge from the tangled growth.

Collected Material – *Yamadori*

The original bonsai trees from both China and Japan were created from collected material and this is still the best (if not the most prolific) source of raw material with character. All the classic old trees would have been growing in the wild for many years before they were potted up and kept in the palaces or temples.

A few centuries ago, most of Europe was still covered in trees. Unfortunately, today, good collected material is not as easy to find. However, there are still abandoned railway lines, disused gravel pits, closed-down factory sites, derelict cottage gardens, natural woodland and Forestry Commission plantations to be explored. Miles of hedgerow are vandalized by removal each year and those hawthorn, hazel, blackthorn and beech stumps must have gone somewhere. Trees that have grown in cracks and were stunted by lack of good soil, munched by animals or

Rescue mission complete: the restyled and re-potted tree needs development but is on its way to becoming a fine tree. (It also resembles the baobab trees on page 32)

placed at the mercy of extreme weather conditions, make ideal bonsai, with more than half of the training already accomplished by nature itself. In the wake of various television 'makeover' programmes, gardens are continually being renovated, and unwanted overgrown shrubs and bushes are often consigned to skips.

Remember that all land, and everything on it, has an owner, and permission must be gained before any trees are dug up and removed. It is essential to follow a few guidelines:

- only remove the tree that you asked for;
- fill in all holes, to ensure that nobody is injured;
- leave the site as clean as you found it, if not cleaner; and
- never remove trees from conservation land – they are there for the enjoyment of others.

Whether it is ethically correct ever to collect from the wild is open to debate. Bonsai clubs often gain permission in spring and autumn to 'hunt' for trees on various areas of woodland – another good reason to join your local club.

Collecting Specimens

When you are searching for trees you need to be eagle-eyed. Even fairly mature examples can be small enough to be lost in the grass. Very small immature trees are usually not worth the effort of lifting as specimen trees because better examples can be obtained from local garden

BELOW LEFT: Collected material is ideal for bonsai styling: they are not easy to spot at first glance, but in this small area of land at the edge of a Forestry Commission plantation in Thetford Forest are birches, beeches, hazels, pines, larch, hawthorn and sycamore. Not all of them are mature but most of them are interesting

BELOW RIGHT: Mark a suitable tree with brightly coloured ribbon: sometimes it can be really difficult to relocate interesting specimens

centres. Collecting seedlings from the wild is quicker than growing from the seed, and they are free, but be warned that the mortality rate among collected seedlings is very high. For group plantings, however, immature trees can be very useful if several of the same species can be found.

When you have located a tree that is of interest but you are not able to lift it immediately, mark it with brightly coloured ribbon so that you can locate it again. Obtain permission to lift the tree and prepare a potting compost that is as close as possible to the tree's present growing medium. Cut a trench around the tree and undercut it by severing the thick taproots that hold it in place. Keep as much soil as possible on the rootball and wrap it in hessian sacking for transportation rather than polythene. Cut off any large unwanted branches. There will be less stress on the tree if it is not required to support branches unnecessarily.

It could be beneficial to the newly lifted tree to have its roots soaked in a dilute solution of specialist rooting hormones such as Super Thrive before being potted. This might alleviate some of the stress suffered by the tree during the lifting process. If this is not possible, make sure that the tree does not dry out and protect it from strong sunlight until it shows signs of recovery. If the tree is really large, storage crates or 'muck' buckets with drainage holes cut into them make very good alternative and inexpen-

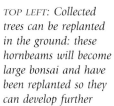

TOP LEFT: *Collected trees can be replanted in the ground: these hornbeams will become large bonsai and have been replanted so they can develop further*

TOP MIDDLE: *Work has already begun on this collected hawthorn but it will still be a long time before its roots are cut back and it is replanted into a bonsai pot*

TOP RIGHT: *A wide variety of large collected trees waiting for styling: plastic storage crates and wooden boxes make ideal 'plant pots' for collected trees*

MIDDLE LEFT: *Neglected gardens can produce remarkable material: shrubs with single stems are not always easy to find but this potentilla was found in the garden of an old cottage that was about to be demolished. It has been in training as a chumono-sized tree for the last ten years*

LOWER MIDDLE LEFT: *Trunk detail and flower (LOWER LEFT) of the potentilla shown above; the trunk shows a range of colours and textures*

MIDDLE RIGHT: *Collected chumono-sized hedgerow blackthorn (Prunus spinosa, or sloe), with flowers and fruit*

Collected hedgerow privet (Ligustrum lucidum) (TOP), with flowers (BELOW RIGHT): the trunk (BELOW LEFT) of this large tree has been extensively carved to create the impression of a hollowed oak

tree. Although the restyled tree will give the basic outline of a mature tree, it will still require time and patience before the illusion of age is complete.

For bonsai styling, garden-centre trees are usually cut down to the size you want them to be rather than having to grow up to it, as is the case when growing from seed. There may be some minor problems in hiding pruning scars but many of the trees will already have thickened and interesting trunks.

For your first attempts at designing, the best results will come from a deciduous tree such as pyracantha or quince, or one of the small-leafed evergreen cotoneasters. These are trees that are shaped by pruning rather than by wiring and the branch structure is clearly visible in the winter months. If you want to develop wiring skills, choose a juniper. Some can be very prickly but good results can be quickly obtained using the basic skills described here.

The 'bargain' area of the garden centre is the place to start looking, not just because there are considerable savings to be made but because some of these trees will have suffered character-building hardships. Twisted trunks and bent branches are not good for garden trees but they

sive 'flowerpots'. If further development of the trunk is needed, plant the tree back in the ground until it has reached the desired size.

The disturbance from lifting will have been traumatic for the tree and in a few weeks, when the tree has settled and has started to produce new roots, it will need feeding intensively if it is to establish new shoots. It may be two or three years before the tree is strong enough to endure radical restyling but spectacular results can be achieved.

Garden-Centre Material

Some trees have large leaves but spectacular spring colour in their flowers: cherry (LEFT); camellia (TOP); magnolia (RIGHT)

Next to buying a tree that has already had bonsai training or collecting a mature tree from the wild, garden-centre material is the next best alternative for creating the illusion of a mature tree in the shortest time. The basic outline of a bonsai can be obtained with just a few hours' or, in some cases, just a few minutes' work, and many years are saved in the development of the

are wonderful for bonsai. Consider the tree. How could it look with some training? The same criteria used for buying bonsai trees should be employed for finding a tree to work on. Look for small leaves, an interesting trunk line, and well-placed branches that are fairly close together. Avoid trees that have thin trunks and very large gaps between branches. It may be possible to get them to bud back but it is easier to find another tree than to go through all that work. Look for bushy, thick-trunked trees with lots of branches that open up endless possibilities for styling.

Trees with large leaves are far from ideal but flower lovers should not disregard them entirely. Some trees, such as cherry, camellia and magnolia, may have large leaves but their spring colour is spectacular and they can be placed out of sight once flowering has finished.

Others, such as wisteria, develop untidy tendril-like shoots but are also worth considering, if only for their spring flowers. Really mature specimens of wisteria are hard to find in garden centres and it may take many years before it flowers. Some flowering trees and shrubs such as azaleas and rhododendrons have small-leafed forms and offer a good alternative to their larger-leafed relatives.

Most of the trees and shrubs found in garden centres have been field-grown and potted up only for resale. This means that they have had room to stretch and grow and develop a trunk but it also means that they may not have a comprehensive root system. If you can, tap the plant out of its pot and check that it has a good root system before you purchase it. It will have been planted fairly deeply in the pot, so the root flare will not be evident, but inspection of the visible roots will give some idea of what to expect.

Free-style juniper (Juniperus communis) in a Chinese pot, developed from a bargain-area tree. This tree has been trained by pruning for ten years and is allowed to follow its own path

Garden-centre Cedar Deodar (Cedrus deodara) being trained in semi-cascade style in a large training pot

Air Layering

Air layering is a way of encouraging the higher branches of trees or shrubs to root while they are still attached to the parent plant. It is also a way of guaranteeing that new trees have

TOP RIGHT: Branches of existing bonsai trees can be air layered to make new trees. Air layering can also be used to encourage roots to form further up a trunk. The top of this lovely maple (RIGHT) needs to be removed to improve the tree's appearance and provides the opportunity for another tree to be created through air layering. The trunk of the collected beech (BOTTOM) has been air layered in a kill-or-cure exercise

Even those garden centres that stock a wide range of trees may have more specimens of the most popular species than of lesser-known ones. If there is only one tree available of the kind you want, don't buy it just because it is there. If it does not have the right characteristics, revise your plans and work on another species of tree until the one you want is available. It will lead to less disappointment in the end.

If you aim to create a tree in a particular style, select your tree very carefully. Do not try to force a tree into a style into which it would never have developed naturally. If the tree has a sturdy upright trunk, it is pointless trying to make it into a cascade tree. If the tree has a distinct lean, or its trunk has a sharp bend, it is not worth trying to turn it into a formal upright. Be philosophical, listen to the tree as well as looking at it, and revise your plans again.

For a list of garden-centre trees suitable for bonsai training, *see* page 106. Detailed instructions on the procedure to be followed for creating a bonsai from garden-centre material start on page 141.

Procedure for air layering a trunk or branch

2. Carefully cut out all the bark in the marked area, making sure that the cut is deep enough to go through the cambium. Remember to leave the thin strip on pines.

1. Using a water-based marker, mark out an area on the branch that is at least as wide as the diameter of the branch so that the area to be cut is clearly defined. If the area is too small, the bark will merely grow over it again rather than produce roots. As rooting takes place fairly quickly on deciduous trees, all the bark encircling the branch should be removed. On coniferous trees, where rooting can take such a long time, it may be better to mark out a very thin strip of bark on the underside of the branch through which nutrients can still flow. This may make the rooting process a little longer but there is far less chance of the branch dying. Remember that roots form at the top of the cut not at the bottom of it.

3. Cover the whole area with hormone rooting compound. Liquid rooting compounds are easiest to apply under these conditions. Alternatively, soak the sphagnum moss in Super Thrive or a similar root-promoting agent.

4. Soak the sphagnum moss in water and cover the whole of the cut area. Secure the moss in place with raffia or string.

5. Cover the area with polythene to keep the sphagnum moss in place and to stop it drying out. (Clingfilm is ideal for this purpose, especially the thicker type that is suitable for use in microwave ovens.) Leave the polythene undisturbed until roots can be seen through it.

Procedure for air layering a trunk or branch *continued*

6. Check the ensemble regularly to ensure that the polythene is still intact and that the moss has not dried out. Birds will sometimes peck through the polythene in the hope of reaching bugs; covering the ensemble in black plastic will discourage them.

7. Rooting begins on deciduous trees much earlier than on coniferous trees. Continue to check regularly that the moss has not dried out.

8. Wait until the new roots are clearly visible through the polythene before severing the branch from the tree.

9. Sever the branch and then plant it in a suitable pot. Remember that it still has a scant root system and will need to be protected. Allow the new tree to develop a comprehensive root system before attempting to style it as a bonsai.

---

exactly the same characteristics as their parents. It can take many years to get seed-grown trees such as crab apple and hawthorn to flower; laburnums have been known to refuse to flower after twenty years of care. An air layer taken from a tree that is already mature enough to flower will itself flower as soon as it is established. Branches of up to 2in (5cm) in diameter can be dealt with in this way and it is a much faster route to acquiring bonsai material than either seeds or cuttings.

Air layering is also useful for producing a new set of roots on the trunk of a bonsai tree where the trunk is too long or has ugly faults that cannot be rectified. With forethought, new trees can also be obtained from branches that are due to be severed from existing bonsai trees during restyling. If time permits (in bonsai design, time should always permit), a new tree could be obtained from material that was too thick to use as a cutting and would have been discarded or trimmed into smaller pieces. As in all these cases, the purpose of the exercise is to produce roots where there were none before. The procedure is the same.

The process of air layering involves removing a wide circle of bark from a branch (ring barking), thereby eliminating its normal source of nutrients and forcing it either to re-root or die. As bark is removed in a ring around the

Semi-cascade and slanting style junipers (Juniperus squamata 'Meyeri'), air layered from garden shrub. Air layering is a method of rooting branches that are still attached to the parent plant

branch, rooting should also occur all around the branch, giving the even root flare that is needed for a good bonsai tree. It is important to remember that roots will appear at the top of the cut area, not at the bottom. The cut area is immediately treated with a hormone rooting compound and covered with a moisture-retaining material, usually fresh sphagnum moss, which is then wrapped in polythene to keep the moisture in while rooting progresses. Deciduous trees root fairly easily in this manner but coniferous trees can take two years to produce roots even with the aid of rooting compounds.

Before starting, select the branch to be air layered carefully so that all the effort expended is worthwhile. What starts off as a branch will soon be a trunk and it is helpful if it already has some bonsai-type characteristics before you begin. Start the process in the spring when the branch has come into leaf. If there are no leaves to support, the tree might think that the branch has no purpose and will allow it to die rather than root.

Growing from Cuttings

General Principles

Growing trees from cuttings is probably the most common method of propagating bonsai, and faster than air layering. Smaller material is produced initially as cuttings are generally taken as shoots rather than branches. Cuttings are available throughout the summer from garden trees and shrubs or from existing bonsai trees when they are pruned to shape. Participants at bonsai club workshops often have bags of unwanted shoots cut from rare or expensive tree species and will give them away freely to anyone who wants to use them for cuttings. Deciduous trees root far more easily than coniferous trees, and it is almost impossible to get pines to root from cuttings but junipers root well.

Cuttings can be taken as soft greenwood in the spring, semi-ripe wood in late summer or as hardwood in late autumn. Greenwood cuttings root the most easily but they also rot the most easily, and losses are high. Hardwood cuttings are not prone to rot but can take a very

If cuttings are not going to be planted straight away, put them in a polythene bag to discourage moisture loss

long time to form roots. If you just want to have a go at growing cuttings, opt for semi-ripe cuttings in summer from wood that has lost its greenness and is beginning to harden.

Choose the cuttings carefully and use those that look as though they will ultimately have the desired characteristics. Trees rarely come true to type from seed but cuttings carry all the characteristics of the parent plant. Coniferous cuttings root better if they have been pulled from the parent plant with a small heel of hardwood attached. Alternatively, use a cutting of about 4–6in (10–15cm) long that has been cut just below a leaf node. Use a sharp knife rather than scissors, as scissors tend to crush the stem. If the cuttings are not going to be dealt with straight away, put them in a polythene bag as soon as they have been cut so that they do not wilt too much.

Whatever the time of year or condition of the cutting, if it is from an interesting tree or a species which you don't have, it is worth popping it in a pot just to see what comes of it. The success rate from cuttings can be fairly low, so plant up many more than you require.

Healthy-looking greenwood Zelkova cuttings prepared from shoots pruned from the tree pictured on page 55

<table>
<tr><th colspan="3" align="center">Equipment checklist: growing from cuttings</th></tr>
<tr><td>Item</td><td>Alternative</td><td>Purpose</td></tr>
<tr><td>Cuttings</td><td></td><td>For propagation</td></tr>
<tr><td>Hormone rooting powder</td><td></td><td>To assist rooting</td></tr>
<tr><td>Compost mixture of peat and
   grit or peat and perlite</td><td>Seed compost</td><td>In which to plant the cutting</td></tr>
<tr><td>Terracotta pot or wooden seed tray</td><td>Plastic seed tray</td><td>In which to plant cuttings</td></tr>
<tr><td>Dibber</td><td>Pencil or chopstick</td><td>Making holes to take the cuttings</td></tr>
<tr><td>Plant labels</td><td></td><td>For identification</td></tr>
<tr><td>Permanent marker</td><td>Ballpoint pen</td><td>For naming species</td></tr>
</table>

If they all take, share them with friends; if they all fail, you'll have to hope that friends will share their successes with you!

Procedure

For deciduous trees, prepare the cuttings by removing the lower pairs of leaves, again using a sharp knife, and reduce any remaining leaves to about a third of their original size. This will cut down on transpiration and moisture loss. Rooting is aided if the stem is slightly damaged and pulling off the lower shoots on coniferous cuttings is advisable. As an alternative, in both coniferous and deciduous cuttings, small wounds can be cut on either side of the cutting or a slither of wood can be cut from one side.

When the cuttings have been prepared, dip them in a rooting compound and plant them up in a suitable pot or tray. The tray should be deep enough to accommodate the cuttings comfortably, and of a porous material that will not encourage stem rot or dry out too quickly. A home-made tray of treated wood or one of terracotta is ideal but a plastic seed tray will suffice. The cuttings need a free-draining and airy planting medium; a mixture of equal parts peat and grit or peat and perlite will encourage root growth.

Provide a drainage layer in the tray of grit, crocks or polystyrene. Using a dibber or a pencil, make evenly spaced holes in the planting medium, insert the bottom third of each cutting and gently firm it in place. When placing the cuttings make sure that there is sufficient space between them so that air can freely circulate. Water thoroughly, spray with a fungicide and protect from pests by adding a thin layer of horticultural grit. Do not be tempted to over-water; only water the cuttings again when the compost shows signs of drying out.

For varieties that are similar and not easily identifiable from each other, label the rows of cuttings with a weatherproof marker. If the cuttings are of a species that are very difficult to root, it may be necessary to provide bottom heat through an electrically heated propagator.

When the cuttings are showing signs of having rooted, pot them up individually. With some species this may be a matter of weeks; others may take up to a year before rooting. Leave the potted tree for another year to develop a strong set of roots before starting to train it. Unlike trees that have been grown from seed, root growth should have developed all around the cutting making it ideal for later bonsai development. A flatter root system can be encouraged when the rooted cutting is potted up by placing a thin piece of slate lower down in the pot. Do not be tempted to do this at the cutting stage as it will hinder root growth rather than help it.

Growing from Seed

Unless you want to grow a large number of trees, or long for something exotic that you are unable to obtain in any other way, growing from seed can be an unnecessarily lengthy way to get a bonsai tree. Patience is required in bonsai, but germination of some seeds is measured in years rather than months and the success rate can be very low. Cross-fertilization sometimes takes place and seeds do not always come true to type; the seeds of a small-leafed variety may, for example, revert to a large-leafed monster. Even after the seeds have germinated

Procedure for growing trees from semi-ripe cuttings

1. Prepare a suitable free-draining planting medium using a mixture of equal parts peat and grit or peat and perlite.

2. Prepare a suitable pot or tray by placing a layer of drainage material in the bottom and then adding the planting material.

3. Prepare coniferous cuttings by pulling away the lower shoots. For broadleaf cuttings, cut off the lower pairs of leaves and reduce the size of existing leaves by two-thirds. Dip each cutting in hormone rooting compound.

4. With a dibber or pencil, make holes in the planting medium and insert the lower third of the cutting. Label the cuttings if they are not easily distinguishable from each other. Water well and spray with a fungicide.

5. Adding a layer of horticultural grit to the surface of the planting medium may discourage some pest attacks.

6. When the cuttings have rooted, pot them up individually. Let the cutting develop a good root system before starting bonsai training.

Seedling trees can be found already sown in your flowerpots and flowerbeds. This oak seedling (TOP LEFT) has germinated from a squirrel-planted acorn, the cotoneaster and holly (LOWER LEFT and TOP RIGHT) from bird droppings, and the pine (LOWER RIGHT) from wind-blown seed

and been potted up it can be several more years before the tree is large enough to work on.

Despite the disadvantages, growing from seed can bring a great feeling of satisfaction, especially if some ultra-desirable sport is produced, which could later be used for cuttings. One other benefit is that the precise age of each tree is known. If you are in a hurry, go for the garden-centre tree but if time is no object growing from seed can be very rewarding.

Pre-germinated seed can be bought from specialist outlets and this can be a good way of growing seedlings, particularly maples for group plantings. However, remember to buy them at regular intervals rather than all at once, otherwise all your trees will be the same size and age. In group plantings, this makes perspective impossible. The same applies to growing from seed yourself; stagger the sowings so that you have trees of different ages.

Look around your own flowerbeds and patio planters to see what has already been sown there naturally by incontinent birds or forgetful squirrels. These garden areas regularly provide seedlings of beech, oak, sycamore, hawthorn, cotoneaster, rowan, blackthorn, yew and pine and, occasionally, larch and field maple. Haw-

thorn takes up to two years to germinate so if you find any seeds that have already sprouted you are several years ahead of the process. Simply pot them up.

Somewhere close by, seedlings of whatever trees are growing in the neighbourhood can usually be found. If they are not in your garden they may be in that of a neighbour, who might treat them as weeds and throw them out. The success rate of seedlings collected from the garden or immediate locality is much higher than it is for those collected from the wild. Also, they can often be left *in situ* so that the roots and trunk can develop further while branches can be selectively pruned to shape, which is a distinct advantage.

Seeds of native trees are conditioned to germinate in the spring after lying in cold, wet ground during the winter months. Autumn is, therefore, naturally the best time for sowing seeds as well as for collecting them. (For a more detailed outline of the various seed forms, *see* page 27) If the seed is going to be sown within a few days it should be kept at room temperature. If sowing is to be delayed, keep the clean seed in the fridge where it will remain cold but not frozen.

Equipment checklist: growing from seed		
Item	**Alternative**	**Purpose**
Fresh tree seeds	Dried tree seeds	For germination
Wooden or terracotta seed tray	Plastic seed tray or flowerpot	In which to plant the seeds
Compost mixture of peat and perlite	Potting compost	In which to plant the seeds
Horticultural grit	Grit	To cover the seeds and prevent stem rot in the seedlings
Plant labels		For identifying seedlings if more than one type is sown
Permanent marker	Ballpoint pen	For marking labels

Put pine and larch cones in a paper bag in a warm place to encourage them to shed their seeds

LEFT: Leave some seedling trees in the ground to grow on and thicken the trunk and branches. The top of the tree can be shaped and pruned while the roots and trunk are developing

The coating of winged seeds such as those of the maple can be easily rubbed away with the fingers but seeds that are covered in fleshy fruit need to be cleaned thoroughly if they are not to rot. This can be achieved by scraping away as much fruit as possible and then soaking the seed in a jar or water for a couple of days until the fruit is soft enough to wash off. Soaking has another good use; good seed sinks whereas empty seed cases float. All floating seed should be thrown away as it will not germinate.

Coniferous seeds need different treatment. Cones that are already open have shed their seeds so collect cones when they are still closed. They will open by themselves eventually, but the process can be accelerated. To collect seeds from pine and larch, place the cones in a paper bag in a warm place; the cones will soon open and the seed will collect in the bottom of the bag. Cones of cedars need to be immersed in hot water and left to soak until they open and the seeds are released.

Hard-coated seeds such as those of beech and oak need to be nicked or scarified to allow germination to occur. A small section of the seed can be filed away or the seed can be nicked with a sharp knife to allow moisture to enter the seed and germination to begin. With small seeds, such as pine, where nicking or scarifying is not feasible, the germination process can be started by vigorously shaking the seeds about in a jar that has been lined with sandpaper.

If dried seeds are being sown out of season, in the summer for example, they will need to be tricked into thinking that winter is finishing and spring is just arriving. This is done by a process called stratification. The seeds will have to be soaked for a couple of weeks to rehydrate them and then kept in the fridge for a month or so to simulate winter conditions before they can be sown. If they are planted straight from the packet they are unlikely to germinate before the following spring, by which time they may have rotted away.

Germinating seeds need air as well as moisture and a light growing medium. A mixture of peat and perlite is ideal. Once sown, the seeds of all native trees can be kept outside in a cold frame or in a cold greenhouse until they germinate. Cover them with netting to protect them from hungry or inquisitive wildlife. Once they have germinated and been pricked out and potted up they should be sprayed with a fungicide to protect them from disease.

Unlike trees produced from air layering or cuttings, those grown from seed tend to have one long taproot rather than an even spread of finer roots. As a flatter root spread is what is required, the taproot should be cut back as far as is feasible when the seedling is potted up. At the same time, pinch out the growing tip to encourage the seedling to grow short and bushy rather than tall and thin.

Trees grown from seed tend to have long taproots, which will need cutting back before potting on

Procedure for sowing from seed

1. Prepare a seed tray of suitable size. It is perfectly acceptable to plant several species of tree in one tray but make sure that each type and variant is clearly marked. Seedlings can wither quickly if they are too dry but they rot easily if they are too wet, so a seed tray of a porous material is useful. A simple home-made wooden tray is ideal or a terracotta pan if one is available, but a plastic seed tray or flowerpot will serve the purpose.

2. Prepare a growing medium: a mixture of peat and perlite is ideal, as it is light and moisture-retentive but drains well.

4. Mark out channels for the seeds and label them. Add a fine layer of sharp sand on top of the compost to make it easier to see small seeds.

5. Sow the seeds carefully, cover them with sieved compost and then add a layer of horticultural grit. Water the planted seeds thoroughly with a mist spray or very fine rose so that they are not disturbed. Only water them again when the compost is drying out. Avoid the temptation to over-water.

6. Wait for germination. This could take up to two years for some species, so be sure to protect the seeds from predatory birds and animals.

7. After germination, cut back the taproot and pinch out the growing tip before potting up.

3. Put a drainage level of crocks, grit or polystyrene in the bottom of the seed tray and add the compost.

Root-over-rock cotoneaster, developed from a flowerbed seedling for fifteen years, planted in a drilled pudding basin

(RIGHT) These shohin-sized larch are fifteen-year-old flowerbed seedlings

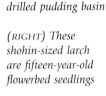

II
Caring for the Tree

5 Tools and Pots

General Principles

There are tools and pots made to fit all purposes in bonsai; the best are those that have been imported from Japan. The size and type of tools you need depends upon the style of trees that you wish to grow. If you have a passion for very small trees, you will not need heavy cutters and power tools, and small pots are easily located. However, if large trees with vast areas of deadwood appeal, then a very wide range of specialist tools and custom-made pots may be required.

Japanese tools are strong, reliable and razor-sharp, and very expensive; consequently, they are items to be acquired over time. Less expensive imports are available, but they are seldom as satisfactory. In the short term, with the exception of knob-cutters, there is a household alternative for almost every tool, and a home-made alternative can be found for most training pots. The time to invest heavily in expensive tools is when the pastime has metamorphosed into an obsession, then tools and pots can head a list of desirable presents.

Tools

Cutting Tools

Scissors of various sizes serve a multitude of purposes, from trimming shoots to cutting back roots. They do not have to be of a specific design but they do have to be very sharp. Long-handled scissors allow access to difficult areas and heavy-duty scissors can tackle most thick roots when re-potting.

Knob-cutters and angled cutters are the only tools for which there is no alternative. They are available in different sizes and can be progressively added to the tool set.

The knob-cutter has a concave edge, which cuts neatly into trunks when pruning branches, leaving a shaped cut that heals over quickly and lies flush to the trunk when it has callused over.

The angled cutter gives a clean cut that is difficult to emulate with scissors and allows access in areas that are not easy to reach with other tools.

For advanced large-size *jins* and *sharis* it is necessary to have an array of sharp cutting instruments. For the carving of hollow-trunk style trees, power tools with specialist drill bits may be necessary. As an alternative, for small *jins* and *sharis*, a sharp knife and a pair of pliers are useful.

Tools and Pots

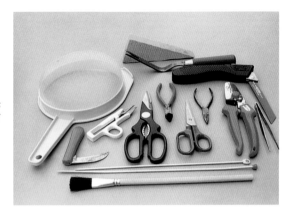

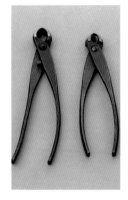

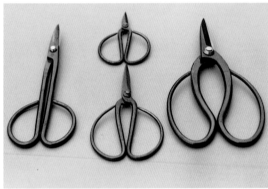

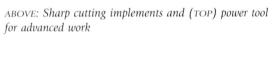

ABOVE: Sharp cutting implements and (TOP) power tool for advanced work

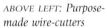

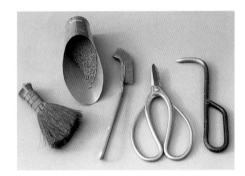

ABOVE LEFT: Purpose-made wire-cutters

ABOVE RIGHT: Various tools for re-potting including a home-made root-hook

Purpose-made wire-cutters for bonsai have a small but very strong cutting edge that is set at the end of the cutter. Avoid using alternatives that have a side cutting action as they may cause damage to the tree.

Re-Potting Tools

In addition to scissors, root hooks and chop-sticks are very useful for untangling roots when re-potting trees and heavy-duty root-pruning scissors can cut through the toughest of roots. A scoop will help with the application of com-posts and a soft brush can be used to smooth the surface of the compost after re-potting is complete. A stiff brush is used for polishing trunks and surface roots to enhance their appearance.

Miscellaneous Tools

A turntable is a must to enable you to view the tree from all angles when working on it. Imported Japanese turntables are either ceramic or made of metal and often have a brake. Alternatives, such as appliance turntables can be used and for large trees a turntable made from a discarded office chair is ideal.

A wraparound tool pouch of synthetic material or leather is ideal for protecting your tools and for taking them to workshops. Place all sharp tools in the pouch handle first, to protect both the pouch and you from damage. An ordinary tool box is invaluable in keeping tools together and to protect them from damage.

Wedges are useful for putting under one side of a pot to assess whether a change of angle would enhance the appearance of the tree.

(LEFT) *Japanese ceramic turntable;* (LOWER LEFT) *Appliance turntable;* (RIGHT) *Turntable made from a discarded typist's chair*

Tweezers and snippers are useful for light pruning and for removing needles from pine trees and dead scales from junipers. A foldaway saw is easily transported and useful for pruning thick branches or cutting off air layers. Small trowels are used for laying moss at the base of the finished tree.

When large cuts are made in trunks and branches it is advisable to cover the wound with a sealant to prevent rot and infection from entering. Hormone rooting compounds are useful for cutting and for air layering and lime sulphur is used for preserving deadwood on *jins* and *sharis*. A toothbrush is a useful applicator and doubles as a stiff brush for cleaning. Rubber gloves are useful when dealing with junipers, a species to which may people have an allergic reaction. As it is necessary to screen bonsai composts to remove dust particles, a sieve with a variety of screens is useful.

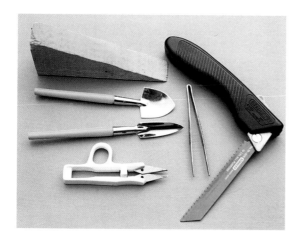

LEFT: *Various miscellaneous tools, from a wedge to a foldaway saw*

Care of Tools

Get into a routine with the care of tools. Always remember to put them away carefully and to clean them first, especially if they have been used on diseased or ailing trees.

Keep the tools sharp and oil them regularly to avoid rust. Remember to move them out of the way when mist-spraying a tree. Never force a tool. If it is inadequate for the job in hand, either use a stronger tool or find an alternative. Japanese bonsai tools are not only extraordinarily sharp but also very brittle and do not easily withstand being dropped on a hard surface.

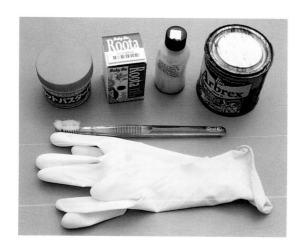

A Place to Work

When working on trees, especially when re-potting, you need a place away from strong sun

Wound sealant, rooting hormones, lime sulphur, a useful applicator (a toothbrush), and protective gloves

71

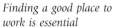

Finding a good place to work is essential

and drying winds. Find somewhere to keep your growing stock of tools, pots and equipment. A bonsai-devoted garden shed is wonderful, but if that is not possible a small area of a shed or garage will suffice. Even a broom cupboard could be commandeered. When the weather is good, take advantage of it and do your pruning outside in the garden.

Pots

General Principles

There are two types of pot for bonsai trees: the training pot and the display pot. While the tree is still developing it should be in a larger, deeper training pot, which can be made of ceramic, wood or plastic. A 'finished' tree that is becoming ready for display is planted in a much shallower ceramic pot. Ceramic pots can be glazed, but on the outside of the pot only; leaving the inside in its natural state allows roots to grip more easily. If it is properly cared for the tree will not come to harm being left in its training pot until the correct ceramic display pot is found for it.

The art of bonsai seeks a union between the tree and its pot, so the pot should be chosen with great care. The tree should suit the pot, never the other way around. Just as you cannot force a tree into a particular style, you should not try to force a tree to fit a particular pot.

Choosing the correct pot for the tree is an art form in itself and trees usually spend parts of their life in various adequate pots until the 'right' one is found. Look through this book and study the relationship of the trees and their pots. Be critical. Not all of the trees are in suitable pots, mainly because most of them are still in training but also because the 'right' pot has yet to be found. On the premise that where bonsai is concerned time is largely irrelevant, most amateurs are patient and know that the pot they are seeking for their tree will turn up eventually.

The guidelines for the size of pot for a finished tree are as follows:

- the pot should be approximately the same depth as the thickness of the trunk;
- the length of the pot should be approximately two-thirds the height of a tall tree; or
- two-thirds the width of a spreading tree.

These are only guidelines and do not apply equally to all trees. First, the pot must be horticulturally suitable for the type of tree; some trees, such as pines, require deeper pots than other species. The style of tree also affects the choice of pot. Cascade trees need tall pots, whereas groups of trees need very shallow containers if they are to be effective. A rugged tree

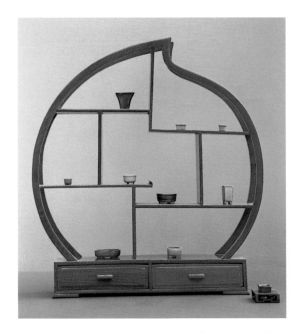

TOP LEFT: A collection of thimble-sized pots on a purpose-built display shelf

TOP RIGHT: Drilled terracotta and stoneware saucers were once the only large 'pots' available

Ceramic pots stored neatly on purpose-built shelves

Pots should have large drainage holes and smaller holes to take retaining wires

needs a rugged pot and a graceful tree needs a pot without harsh contours.

Muted colours are preferable for most bonsai trees, so that they complement the tree rather than compete with it. If attention is drawn away from the tree towards the pot then the pot needs changing. Brighter colours and glazes can be used for trees that have colour of their own; those that flower profusely or those that have highly pigmented foliage. The tiny pots of mame trees are sometimes brightly coloured, patterned and glazed.

Twenty years ago, when bonsai pots were difficult to find, many enthusiasts spent much of their time in kitchen shops seeking out shallow pudding basins that could be drilled. High-fired, frost-proof terracotta saucers from the garden centre proved to be more than adequate as training pots, as they were flat, round and easily drilled. Unfortunately they lacked the short legs of bonsai pots that keep them off the ground and assist drainage. The saucers shown above have been in almost constant use for two decades and, although a wide range of pots is now available, these old 'friends' still make good inexpensive training pots.

Ceramic Pots and Alternatives

Ceramic pots are available in a multitude of sizes, shapes, glazes and colours. Small and medium-sized pots can be bought from garden centres but large pots still need to be bought

Mica pot – an inexpensive alternative to ceramic

from specialist centres or directly from bonsai potters. Pots are available by mail order, although there is a risk that the colour and glaze may not match the catalogue representation. A good pot will have large drainage holes and smaller holes through which retaining wires can be put.

Mica pots are an inexpensive alternative to large ceramic pots. They have a far more realistic ceramic-looking finish than plastic pots and can on occasion pass for the real thing.

Tools and Pots

Plastic pots are acceptable for training

RIGHT: *Hollow-trunk garden privet (Ligustrum) (TOP) and a Trident Maple (Acer buergerianum) (BOTTOM): specialist tools are necessary to create extensive hollow-trunk effects*

A variety of containers can be used as training pots

Plastic pots are far from ideal because they do not 'breathe' and tend to have a shiny surface. However, they are very inexpensive and come in a wide range of shapes and sizes, most of which are suitable for training purposes

As a 'proper' bonsai pot is only really necessary when the tree is finished or to be displayed, a wide range of receptacles is suitable for training purposes. Plastic storage crates, wooden boxes, plastic seed trays and muck buckets can all be utilized for collected and other bonsai material.

Slabs and rocks, although not exactly pots, make very attractive bonsai containers, giving single trees and groups of trees a natural look that is sometimes missing from more formal display pots. Artificial slabs made of fibreglass and high alumina cement are both lightweight and attractive. For details of how to make an artificial slab, *see* Chapter 15 (pages 148–149).

6 Watering, Feeding and Display

General Principles

Water is a matter of life and death to a tree, so the first essential skill to master is the art of watering. Watering is a balancing act; with too little water, the tree will die of drought; too much water will cause it to die of root rot. Most of the tree losses suffered by new bonsai enthusiasts can be attributed to watering problems – usually over-watering rather than under-watering. If a mistake is made with pruning there is a chance to put it right at a later date when new buds appear but, if consistent mistakes are made with watering, it is seldom correctable.

All trees stay in one place, but trees that are growing naturally spread their roots in a search for food and water. Trees confined to small pots are not able to do this and, as constant watering flushes essential minerals from the compost, they need both food and water provided for them on a regular basis if they are to stay healthy. Mame trees require very frequent watering and, even though they are tiny, they need feeding as often as bigger trees. Most beginners not only over-water their trees, they also underfeed them.

The nature and source of the water available for trees is also important. Tapwater may have additives that are intended to protect human health but do little for the health of a tree. In hard-water areas, tapwater contains a high level of lime and salts that not only cause chlorosis in acid-loving plants but also cause white deposits on leaves and pots. If you are unsure whether you are in a hard- or soft-water area, look inside your kettle. If it is furred up with limescale, the water is hard. Water can be neutralized to a degree by letting it stand in a barrel for a few days before using it. This will allow

time for most of the chlorine and other chemical additives to break down or evaporate. Use a fine rose for watering trees and also give the leaves a good covering to keep them free from dust and to dislodge any unwelcome insect visitors.

Only tropical tree species should be kept inside the house. Space must be provided for all other trees in the garden, where they can be admired and kept safe from harm.

Watering

Trees are individual, and not all of them will want the same amount of water. The water needs of trees vary according to their species: pines and junipers are used to more arid conditions than maples and other broad-leafed trees. Trees with large leaves lose more moisture through transpiration than small-leafed and needled species. All these factors have to be taken into account when planning a watering regime.

Look at the compost where the tree is growing. If it consists mainly of coarse granules and is free-draining, watering is far less of a problem, but if it is in hardened clay or dry peat, the situation is different. When bonsai trees have been bought from garden centres they are often in compost that is unsuitable for a European climate. Many will have been in their pots for so long that they will be completely pot-bound.

If the tree is in clay where the granules have broken down into a solid lump, it may initially be difficult to get water to penetrate and reach all of the tree's roots. Clay changes colour when it is wet and it is fairly easy to tell when it is wet or dry. If the tree has been deprived of water for a long time, place the pot in a bowl of water for ten minutes. During this time the clay will absorb all the moisture that it can, and this will penetrate the middle of the rootball. Do not leave it in the water longer than ten minutes, and do not water the tree again until the compost shows signs of having dried out.

When they are dry, peat-based composts contract and pull away from the sides of the pot, and peat is very difficult to re-wet once all the moisture has left it. If normal watering is carried out when it is in this state the water will simply run away and will not penetrate the compost. There is no alternative but to soak the pot in a bowl of water as with hardened clay. In both situations the problem can be solved when the tree is re-potted into a more suitable compost mix (*see* Chapter 8, pages 83–84).

If trees have been over-watered and are suffering, reduce watering immediately, keeping the compost only slightly moist. Check the drainage holes to ensure that they have not become blocked and inspect the benching to see if anything is preventing water from draining away. Check to see if the tree is in too much shade. If the tree shows signs of having root rot, there may be no alternative other than to re-pot. If the tree is already in a free-draining compost mix, re-site the tree to improve drainage further. If the tree dries out too quickly, check if there is too much sun and consider moving the tree into a more shaded area.

During the summer, water the trees in the evening so that they have the night to absorb water before the sun hits them again. If your trees need watering during the winter months, water them in the morning so that they are not left with wet leaves and wet compost during a freezing night. The tree should be watered until water can be seen coming through the drainage holes at the bottom of the pot and should not be watered again until all water has been taken up and the compost has started to dry out. Water the trees lightly using a fine rose and then repeat the process a few minutes later when the first lot of water has been absorbed. In this way, the water should penetrate the rootball instead of just running off.

Surprisingly, it is important to water your trees even when it rains. If the tree has a full canopy of leaves very little rainwater will be able to reach the pot; trees can suffer from drought even in a wet summer.

When there has been excessive rain, which has left the pot continually soaked, measures have to be taken to keep the tree out of harm's way for a while. If possible, pop the tree into an outside covered area, cold frame or ventilated greenhouse. Do not tilt the pot on its side, as this will just cause a big puddle to form in one side of the pot. Water may drain away over the lip of the pot but too much water will be trapped inside. If no cover is available, try a small 'mackintosh' or umbrella of a polythene bag over the pot as a temporary measure.

If you have been on holiday and your trees have suffered from drought and lost their leaves, make yourself a promise to provide an automatic watering system for next year. Do not despair, though; the trees may be leafless, but they are not necessarily dead. Water the tree well and cosset it for a while, and buds will probably appear before too long. Stressed trees will shed their leaves as an act of reducing water loss and increasing the chance of survival. The drought has to be fairly prolonged before a tree will die.

Mist-spray the leaves of both deciduous and coniferous trees. Although they prefer dryer conditions than deciduous trees, conifers do not like their foliage to be too dry. Mist-spraying on a regular basis will increase humidity for the tree without flooding its roots.

Fertilizers

As trees grow, nutrients are taken out of the compost and the health and vigour of the tree will be lost if the tree cannot find a continuing supply of food. In the natural world, if a tree is unable to find food and water, it will simply die and a more vigorous tree will take its place. Do not feed the tree when it is under stress – for example, when it has been newly re-potted or when its roots have been damaged. A tree will not die quickly from lack of food as it would from lack of water.

The luxuriant growth and large leaves sought in garden plants are not encouraged in bonsai, as foliage needs to be in proportion with the size of the tree. Fertilizers that are high in leaf-producing nitrogen are generally discouraged; fertilizers that are used to produce fruit and flowers rather than leaves, such as tomato fertilizers, are preferable. However, in the spring, when buds are bursting, and in the autumn,

when buds are forming, the tree needs a good dose of nitrogen to boost its vitality.

Bonsai growers swear by their own concoctions of fertilizing agents, and seaweed extract, pelleted chicken manure and rapeseed cakes are all used. In these cases the ingredients are organic, but there are enthusiasts who manage to grow prize-winning trees using simple soluble garden fertilizers such as phostrogen. Soluble fertilizers recommended for ericaceous shrubs can be invaluable to give a tonic to ailing azaleas. A weekly addition of soluble fertilizer to the general watering regime will keep the tree in good condition; always use it strictly in accordance with the manufacturer's instructions. Twice the strength will do twice the harm, not twice the good. Also, never use it in a dry state as this may burn the roots and harm the tree.

Both chemical and organic specially made fertilizers are available for bonsai trees, but organic fertilizers are by far the safest to use in the confined space of a bonsai pot. Microbes in the compost break down the fertilizer to release the nutrients in it, and the tree will take up these nutrients only as and when it needs them. When using organic fertilizers there is no need to worry about burning roots or overfeeding. A handful of solid organic fertilizer, such as a mixture of blood, fish and bone, should be added to all bonsai trees in the spring and autumn of each year to help swell the growing buds and increase the vigour of the tree. All the liquid organic fertilizers on the market are useful for bonsai trees if they are mixed as instructed by the manufacturer.

Cakes of organic fertilizer can be left on the surface of the compost and will add nutrients to the compost each time the tree is watered. They are not aromatic and you will need understanding neighbours, but they are easily made. A medium-sized tree will need at least four of these cakes on the compost at any one time during the summer months and they should be replaced on a monthly basis.

Recipe for rapeseed fertilizer cakes

Ingredients:

- 70 per cent rapeseed
- 20 per cent fishmeal
- 10 per cent bonemeal; and
- sufficient water to bind the ingredients into soft balls.

Method:
Mix the rapeseed, fishmeal, bonemeal and water into a consistency that holds together and can be flattened like pastry. Allow it to dry out and then cut it into pieces.

Display

Bonsai trees are meant to be seen at eye level and should be displayed in such a way that the viewer can see them comfortably without having to crouch down. Placing them on stands not only enhances their appearance but also helps to protect them from pests.

Benching set about 4ft (120cm) above the ground is ideal. This is something that can be planned for the future, when you might come to consider the idea of a bonsai area. Tiered shelving is a good compromise. It means that only one of the tiers is at the correct height but it does allow a large number of trees to be shown in a small space.

Simple but attractive stands can be made from concrete blocks and paving stones. Because of problems of balance, without adequate footings they are lower than is ideal but they are inexpensive and require no maintenance.

7 Maintenance Pruning

Trident Maple in a Japanese bonsai centre: even mature trees need a summer haircut

General Principles

Unless it is winter, after just a few weeks your tree will look as though it is in urgent need of a haircut. Neat and tidy spring buds will have opened and then extended into long shoots that stick out in all directions, totally obscuring the lines of the tree. This shaggy-dog look is perfectly normal. It is more marked in young trees that are full of vigour than in mature trees, where the growth is less thrusting, but even mature trees need to have their shape continually controlled. Bonsai trees are not slow growing and constant vigilance is necessary if you are to maintain the illusion of a perfectly formed miniature tree.

The purpose of maintenance pruning is twofold: it will keep the foliage pads compact and also encourage budding, which will increase ramification and add density to the foliage pads. It is completed in two ways that are dependent on the species of the tree: shoots can be either cut off with scissors or pinched out with the fingers. Scissors are used on broadleaf trees and on scale junipers; pinching is used on pines, needle junipers and most conifers. Do not cut or pinch off all the growing shoots from a branch in one fell swoop. If the branch does not have a good reason to send sap to its ends it will not do so and the whole branch may die back.

Although maintenance pruning affects the shape of the tree and is performed continuously throughout the summer, it is not done to alter the tree's basic shape. Removing excessive young growth causes new shoots to form but only in the joints of leaves near the cut or pinch, not further down the branch or on the trunk. If back-budding for development is required,

much harder pruning is needed (*see* Chapter 11).

Whatever pruning is done in one year will affect how the tree will look in the next year, so give thought to where the tree is heading in terms of ramification of branches. If a branch is to be thickened, as is often the case with the lower branches of very young trees, leave the branch completely unpruned and let it extend for a season before cutting it back. The branch has to draw up more sap to feed the extra growth and it will thicken accordingly. The tree will look strange for one year but eventually the effect will be of a branch that looks more mature and has a better balance.

Regardless of the species of tree, cut off or pinch out every shoot that is growing either straight up or straight down from the branch. These shoots will serve no purpose in the tree's development and will have to be removed eventually when they start to interfere with other branches. The same is true of exceptionally long growth on branches that are not required to thicken. If the growth extends beyond the triangular shape of the tree, cut it back, but always make sure that there are other shoots to continue the growth on the branch.

Deciduous Trees

Maintenance Pruning with Scissors

When removing shoots from deciduous trees, scissors are used instead of the fingers as they give a straight clean cut to the shoot rather than crushing it. Although eventually only one set of buds is required from the shoot, it should be cut back to two pairs of leaves from which buds can form. Shoots have a habit of dying back past one pair of leaves and if only one set were left then the whole branchlet would be lost.

Sever the shoot just above a leaf joint leaving a little stub; this will dry and drop off eventually and will reduce the chance of die-back. Do not rush to prune the shoot as soon as the third set of leaves appears. The new shoots that form from the buds will grow parallel to the old branch rather than at an angle to it. Waiting that little bit longer before cutting back the shoot brings more character to the tree by giving sharper angles to the growth.

Shoots that are totally out of proportion with the tree, having become really thick or having long lengths of stem between the leaves (internodes), should also be eliminated. Single oversized leaves should be cut off wherever they appear. If all the leaves on the tree are oversized, this can be dealt with by leaf-pruning.

Once you have gone over the whole tree removing unwanted shoots, you will be amazed at the size of your pile of discarded foliage. A huge amount of growth can take place in a short time and, if the tree is vigorous and healthy, the process will need to be repeated several times.

Leaf-Pruning

Sometimes a tree will produce unexpectedly large leaves, or leaves that are out of proportion to its trunk and branches. On younger trees that are healthy and growing vigorously this problem can be rectified by leaf-pruning. This process means that the tree is artificially defoliated by having all its leaves cut off in early summer. Forcing the tree into making two years' growth in one year is something that should not be undertaken lightly, or repeated regularly. Trees need their leaves for the production of food so the tree should have been well fed, and not newly re-potted, before the process begins.

As with most corrective processes, leaf-pruning has its drawbacks as well as its advantages. The new set of leaves should be much smaller than the first set and may have an enhanced autumn colour but, on the other

Cut back to two pairs of leaves just above a leaf joint but leave a small stub (LEFT); shoots will form in the old leaf joints (ABOVE)

Japanese Maple (LEFT) and larch (RIGHT): in spring, unwanted growth is systematically removed. What is done this year affects how the tree will look next year

ABOVE: *Candidate for leaf-pruning: this is a small-leafed lime but its leaves are still far too big; de-leafing should produce a new set of smaller leaves*

ABOVE RIGHT: *Looking for new buds*

totally out of proportion with the others. Young maples and limes usually respond well to this treatment but it should not be used on the cut-leafed varieties of maples or on slow-growing species such as beech.

Timing is important for this process. It should occur late enough into the summer months for the tree to have set its buds already, but not so late that the new growth does not have time to harden before winter sets in. Depending on the tree and the climate, mid-June to mid-July is the best time to de-leaf a tree.

The leaves must be *cut* off, not pulled off. If they are pulled off, there is a great possibility that the new buds will come off with the leaves, which will defeat the whole purpose of the exercise. Without leaves, the tree will not lose any water through transpiration and a careful feeding and watering regime should be established. The tree will need enough feeding to

hand, defoliating the tree is extremely debilitating and there is the chance that it might not recover from the trauma. On really aged specimens, leaf size should be controlled through feeding and watering, not by removal of any leaves other than the odd one or two that are

Procedure for leaf-pruning a tree

1. Check that the tree has set new buds before any leaves are removed.

2. Start cutting off the leaves. Make the cut just below the leaf blade, leaving all of the leaf stalk attached to the branch.

4. New, smaller leaves should start to appear after four to six weeks.

3. Without its leaves, the tree will need careful feeding and watering. When the leaves have been removed it is easy to see the branch structure and to work on the rectification of any faults. Trim back any long growth. There is no point in making the tree produce unwanted leaves.

keep it healthy until the new leaves have appeared, but not so much that the leaves grow back as large as they were before the process began. If the tree is in a free-draining soil mix, watering will not be a problem but, if this is not the case, check the compost to make sure that water is really needed before adding moisture.

Coniferous Trees

Pruning by Finger-Pinching

Conifers also need some attention throughout the summer, but most of their pruning is done in late spring when all the buds have opened and the shoots are beginning to extend. If left unchecked, this growth quickly obscures the shape of the tree.

Needle junipers, hemlocks, cedars and most other coniferous trees can have their spring growth checked by pinching out with the fingers when it is still very short. To pinch out a shoot, simply hold the base of the shoot in one hand, to make sure that it is not pulled away from the branch, and gently tug at the shoot with the other hand until the shoot separates.

Junipers have both juvenile and adult foliage. Immature foliage is in the form of short, spiky, needle-like scales and the mature foliage is in the form of soft scales. Most junipers carry both adult and juvenile foliage and it is almost impossible to prevent the juvenile foliage from appearing. The San Jose Juniper permanently carries both types; if a uniform tree is desired, it is better to remove the adult foliage and leave the juvenile foliage on the tree.

Scissor-Pruning Adult Foliage of Junipers

The adult foliage of junipers is in the form of soft scales and, compared with the needle-type growth, is very slow-growing. Pinching of scales will remove not only this year's growth but much of last year's growth too. Pruning is better done with scissors. Instead of taking off the growing tip of every shoot, remove only the shoot that needs shortening. Care should be taken to ensure that there is a remaining shoot to take over as a growing point.

The attractive bright green shoots of the cedar (ABOVE) elongate quickly and obscure the shape of the tree (BELOW)

ABOVE LEFT AND RIGHT: Pinching out shoots on a juniper: pinching out the growing tips of conifers keeps the foliage pads compact and encourages density

Scissor-pruning the adult scale foliage of junipers: scales are too slow-growing to withstand pinching and should be pruned with scissors

Maintenance Pruning of Pines

Pines can often produce a whorl of 'candles' at the end of a shoot. These not only look immature but, if left unchecked, can also cause an unsightly lump to form on the branch. In mature pines these candles are not a problem,

Pines can produce whorls of unwanted branches. If there are three or more candles on a branch (MIDDLE), leave only two of the less vigorous ones to continue growing (RIGHT)

as the growth of the tree is more controlled, but in less mature trees the candles are numerous and grow rapidly.

If there are three or more candles at the end of the branch, the most vigorous candles should be removed, leaving only two smaller candles to extend. These less vigorous candles are more likely to give the more favoured shorter growth and smaller needles. Leaving three candles will result in an unrealistic T-bar growth on the branch. With two candles, one will continue to grow as the main branch and the other will become a side branch.

There is no rush to pinch out the unwanted candles, as they are drawing sap into the branch, but they should be removed completely before they interfere with other branches on the tree. When the growth on the candles that are to be retained is between 1 and 2in (2.5–5cm) long, the candle should pinched in half. Hold the bottom half of the candle to make sure that it

is not pulled away from the branch and tug at the top half until it separates. Alternatively, simply bend the shoot until it snaps cleanly in half.

De-Needling pines

The needles on pines only live for a few years and then drop off naturally, so there is no harm in hurrying the process by removing them manually. Shoots have needles on them, and branches do not. If needles are left on the 'branches' of your tree, they will look like twigs. Needles can be pulled from underneath the branches, where no further buds are required. However, in areas where new buds are hoped for, the needles should be cut very short with scissors, leaving the embryonic bud that is between the needles to develop.

Candles should be halved by pinching when they are between 1 and 2in (2.5–5cm) long

8 Re-Potting

General Principles

The prospect of re-potting a bonsai tree can be daunting. The tree has been cared for, watered, fed and trimmed; now, it has to be taken out of its pot, have its roots cut back and be put back in its pot again. However, by following a few basic guidelines and working quickly, risks can be minimized and the tree will quickly recover, relishing its new compost.

The first rule of re-potting a bonsai tree is preparation; the second and third rules are also preparation. The importance of getting everything ready before you start cannot be stressed enough. Work inside your house or workshop on a cool day, away from any breeze, which might accelerate the tree's drying-out process. Avoid distractions. The fine white hairs on tree roots dry out and die very quickly once they are exposed to the air and irreparable damage can be caused in the time it takes to answer the telephone.

Why Re-Pot?

Trees are re-potted for several reasons: to renew vigour; to encourage the growth of fine feeding roots and to enhance aesthetic qualities, with improvement of the root flare and a possible change of position or pot. Re-potting is a time for renewal and refinement. Bonsai trees may need to be partially root-bound to restrict their growth but if they are totally root-bound then they will suffer. Keeping the visible parts of the tree healthy needs a correspondingly healthy root system; the condition of one reflects the condition of the other.

Only the minute hairs just behind the root's growing tip take up nutrients; as these roots are

Re-potting allows the position of the tree to be changed: a brick has been placed under this tree's pot, improving its viewing angle. When the tree is eventually re-potted, its roots will be adjusted to accommodate the change

short-lived, they have to be constantly renewed, which is why the tree continuously extends its roots until they curl round the pot. Without regular pruning, roots become longer and thicker instead of becoming denser. Eventually the pot becomes full of roots, which seriously affects their efficiency and the growth rate of the tree. Re-potting the tree gives it space in which the whole process can be repeated. New growing tips will be formed on the roots, enabling them to function properly and take up moisture and nutrients again.

Re-potting may also be carried out because the tree's existing pot may not be of the right style, colour, depth or width. Re-potting the tree in a more suitable pot, and rearranging any crossed or misplaced roots, may enhance the tree's overall appearance.

When to Re-Pot

The best time to re-pot all varieties of trees is in late winter or early spring, when the tree is beginning to become active but before its buds

Tight buds on a small-leafed lime (LEFT) and open buds on a hornbeam (MIDDLE): if the buds have broken open and the leaves can be seen then it is too late to re-pot the tree and it should be left until the autumn

TOP RIGHT: Visible tree roots say it is time to re-pot: the roots of this mountain pine have pushed their way through the surface of the compost and are winding their way around the edge of the pot

have started to break open. On deciduous trees, if leaves can be seen then it is too late to re-pot and the tree should be left until autumn or the following spring. Buds break on different types of trees at different times so it is difficult to say exactly when re-potting should be carried out. Elms come into leaf very early, while others, such as lime, come into leaf much later.

Frost is a great killer of roots. Trees re-potted in midwinter will benefit from dormancy, but will not recover until their roots start growing again in the spring. When a tree has been re-potted it needs to be given tender loving care in protected conditions; subjecting it to winter weather is unlikely to do it much good. Trees that are re-potted in autumn have some time to recover before the bad weather sets in; they should still be protected from frost but not cossetted to such an extent that they think spring had arrived and start growing again. Flowering trees generally respond fairly well to being re-potted in the autumn.

In spring, re-pot deciduous trees first, and then re-pot conifers, leaving the needle junipers until last, as they start growing later than other trees. Never re-pot a deciduous tree in midsummer when it is in full leaf, as it is unlikely to recover from the shock. It is possible, however, to re-pot deciduous trees in the summer if they have first been completely de-leafed through pruning. However, as de-leafing causes stress to the tree, doubling the stress by re-potting is not really advisable unless there is an emergency.

Advice is often given that conifers can be re-potted at almost any time during the growing season but this is only valid in areas of extremely high humidity. In Europe, where conditions in midsummer are fairly arid, resist the temptation to re-pot conifers after the end of May.

How Often to Re-Pot?

This is a difficult question to answer, as everything depends upon the individual tree and its existing circumstances. The tree's variety, age, size, and style, and its present pot are all factors in the decision over whether to re-pot now, or to leave it for another year. Everyone's memory is fallible; keep careful records, so that you know the exact time of every re-potting.

A visual check will tell you whether the tree is suffering in its present state. If roots can be seen poking their way up the sides of the pot or forcing their way through the drainage holes, it is time to do something about it. Any pruning

Rule of thumb guide: re-potting trees		
Type of tree	**When to re-pot**	**How often to re-pot**
Conifers	In early to late spring when growth is evident	Every three to five years
Deciduous	In spring before the buds break open	Every two to three years
Flowering trees	Immediately after flowering or in early autumn	Every one to two years
Fruit trees	In spring before the buds break	Every one to two years
Indoor bonsai	In early spring before the buds break	Every two to three years
Mame tree	Early spring	Every year

or wiring that needs to done to shape the tree should be completed before it is re-potted.

Young trees have vigorous growth and need to be re-potted more frequently than mature trees. Trees in tiny pots quickly outgrow the small space available. If the tree is mature, it can be re-potted into a pot of the same size, but if it is still being developed then it should be moved into a pot of a larger size.

If some of the tree's branches are dying back or it is looking less than perky, this could indicate an inefficient root system, which might be improved by re-potting into a better growing medium. If water pools on the surface of the soil instead of draining through it is also a signal that the tree is in urgent need of re-potting.

Compost for Bonsai

A tree grown in a pot is obviously being kept in unnatural conditions. If it is to remain vigorous and healthy, every effort must be made to make it as comfortable as possible.

It is not advisable to grow a bonsai tree in garden soil as this may contain pests, and it will almost certainly compact and lead to root trouble. Nor is it advisable to use general house-plant potting compost; this is not free-draining, and trees have different needs from house-plants. There are several commercially prepared bonsai soils that can be bought in small bags from garden centres but they tend to be expensive and, as trees have varying requirements, it is better to mix your own. If only one tree needs to be potted, the commercially prepared bags of bonsai compost may be your best bet, however; any 'extras' can be added to suit the tree.

Composition

When deciding which ingredients should go into a bonsai compost mix, consider the terrain in which the tree would naturally be growing (*see* Chapter 2). These are the conditions that will need to be simulated for the tree to be healthy and survive. Pine trees do not like to be too damp, whereas deciduous trees suffer badly from drought. It is not the amount of nutrient in the soil that is important – balanced feeding can replace any deficiencies. Rather, the prime

factor is the relationship between drainage and moisture retention. Tree roots need moisture but they also need air, so any compost that compacts and denies air to the roots should be avoided.

Bonsai composts consist mainly of inorganic substances (those that have never been alive, such as sand, grit or clay), and organic substances that were formed from plant or animal matter, such as peat and bonemeal. Inorganic materials are largely inert and do not nourish the tree. Organic matter is added to the basic mix to suit the tree's nutrient needs and increase the water retention level. Several factors have to be taken into account when deciding on the ratio between inorganic and organic matter in a bonsai compost:

- the type of tree;
- the climatic conditions in which the tree is growing; and
- the size of the drainage holes in the pot.

As composts mix on the first watering it is not necessary to have layers of different potting materials. Tests over the last few years have proven that a tree responds well to a single compost being used throughout the pot. If it is a suitable medium for potting at one level then it is suitable throughout the pot.

If the compost is to be free-draining it needs to have a crunchy consistency, with a high concentration of irregular granules of a hard material that has been sifted to make sure that all small particles and dust have been removed. To test the compost, pick up a handful and squeeze it. If it does not make an audible crunching sound, it is not 'gritty 'enough, and needs more hard particles added to it. Imported akadama clay is ideal for this purpose as it holds moisture well and takes a long time to break down.

Akadama clay, imported from Japan, is hard and has an irregular shape, making it ideal as the major component of bonsai compost

Both inorganic and organic materials are used in bonsai potting compost: a. perlite; b. calcined clay; c. peat; d. akadama; e. red granite; and f. horticultural grit

when they are wet. It also costs less and is more readily available than akadama.

Grit is a suitable, less expensive alternative to clay and mixing the two gives a highly efficient cost-effective base for the potting medium in which most trees can be planted. In Japan, grit is more expensive than readily available clay and many exported bonsai pine trees are planted in grit alone. Red granite chippings are extremely useful as they are inexpensive, stocked by DIY stores and aesthetically pleasing. Other materials such as pumice and vermiculite are suitable for potting purposes, but their bright white or light grey colour jars against the eye and is against the concept of bonsai presentation.

Trees can be planted in inorganic materials alone but they will require a very strict watering and feeding regime. If the drainage holes in the pot are small there should be more inorganic matter in the compost mix, to assist drainage and prevent root rot. If the drainage holes are large, then more organic matter such as peat can be added to the mix.

Moss peat is a useful organic material for bonsai composts as it has a coarse texture. Sedge peat is a bit too granular and sticky. However, as peat is difficult to re-wet once it has become completely dry, and as there are worries over the conservation of peat beds, peat substitutes are often recommended. The problem here is that many of these substitutes, such as coir, are non-acidic and if the tree is of a variety that requires an acidic environment (for example, azalea), some are not suitable. Check the requirements of the tree and the pH level of any chosen substitute before you use it.

If junipers are to be re-potted, the addition of fresh sphagnum moss to the mix can have remarkable effects on the root development of

It also has an irregular shape, which not only increases the surface area over which the roots can grow, but also allows for the vital tiny pockets of air that the roots need. Akadama can be expensive but when the value of the tree is taken into account its cost comes into perspective. It is available in several grades, the best of which is known as 'two line'; 'one line' is of medium quality and 'no line' is a somewhat mediocre product for which better alternatives can be found.

Calcined clay products, such as Biosorb, are also sometimes useful. In the calcining process, clay is heated to a temperature at which both the absorbed and the structural moisture is dried off, leaving it hard and dry. (Before being used for horticultural purposes the main use for baked clay was cat litter, which is why some recommend including cat litter in bonsai compost mixes.) The grains of calcined clay crumble more easily than akadama grains when they are squashed, but they do not go soft

Rule of thumb guide: bonsai composts

Type of tree	Inorganic material	Organic materials
Mountain trees (pine, juniper, etc.)	Three-quarters	One-quarter
Other conifers (larch, spruce, hemlock, etc.)	Two-thirds	One-third
Flowering trees and fruit trees (cherry, pyracantha, quince, etc.)	Half	Half
Deciduous trees	One-third	Two-thirds
Indoor trees	One-third	Two-thirds
Acid-loving trees (azalea, redwood, etc.)	One-quarter	Three-quarters
Mame tree	One-quarter	Three-quarters

Preparing the New Pot

Siftings of peat and clay are not wasted as they can be used for other things: a compound of peat and clay siftings can be used as a base for planting moss

the tree. Cut the moss into small pieces and mix it with the sifted compost. It helps to retain moisture, while keeping the soil open, and the juniper roots will soon locate it and flourish. Moss is also ideal for wrapping around the roots of trees that have damaged root systems and for trees that have been recently lifted from the ground and have scant root systems.

Using and Re-Using Compost

Soil for re-potting should always be used when it is dry, as it is easier to handle and to work down between the roots than when it is wet. If time permits, leave damp compost for a while to dry out. It is also easier to sift if it is dry. The amount of material removed through sifting can be alarming and make you wonder if it is really all worthwhile. It is. The siftings do not have to be discarded, as peat and clay can be moulded together into a putty-like consistency to be used as a base for planting moss or for the rock plant-ing of trees (*see* Chapter 13).

It is possible, but not always advisable, to save old compost and re-use it. If the last tree growing in it was healthy, and was re-potted merely because its roots had outgrown the space available, rather than because it was sick, there is no reason for the compost to be discarded. Remove any old roots that are evident, allow the compost to dry out completely, then sift it to remove any dust residue from peat or broken-down clay. Bag the compost in its dry state and leave it until the following spring to ensure that there were no bugs in it. Mix it with fresh compost in a ratio of up to one-third old compost to two-thirds new compost.

Prepare the new pot in which the tree is to be planted before removing the tree from its old pot. If the tree is to be re-potted back into the same pot, remove the tree from the pot and protect its roots from drying out by putting a polythene bag over them. This will keep the tree safe until the pot is ready and root-pruning can begin.

First, wash the pot thoroughly to remove any spores of fungi or plant diseases that might be lying in wait for the new tree. If you are in a hard-water area, there may be deposits of limescale marring the pot's appearance. These can be removed in several ways other than by the use of excessive elbow grease. Soak the pot overnight in a solution of cream of tartar and hot water or, alternatively, immerse it for an hour in a weak solution of a proprietary kettle descaler. After using chemicals for cleaning, carefully wash the pot again and let it dry out thoroughly before you use it.

Good bonsai pots have large centralized drainage holes and smaller outer holes for drainage and wiring. Unless these holes are covered, soil will slide straight through them on watering and harmful insects will be able to gain easy access to the pot. Cover the holes with plastic screening mesh and hold it in place with wire. If you do not secure the mesh in the pot, it may move about when you are positioning the tree and leave the hole uncovered.

The tree will need to be fixed firmly into the pot to stop it rocking about, which could cause root damage. Take a length of wire and thread

Protect the roots of the tree: roots dry out quickly, so if re-potting is delayed protect the tree's roots with a polythene bag

Examples of plastic screening mesh

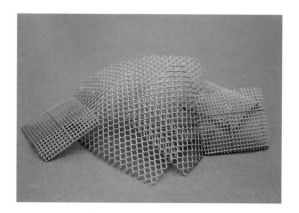

each end through a smaller hole, so that the ends are sticking up above the pot; repeat the process so that you have a length of wire poking up through each of the smaller holes. The retaining wires can easily be removed, if desired, when the tree has become firm in its pot. Simply cut the wire under the pot, trim the ends so that they cannot snag and gently pull the wire up through the roots. When the mesh is in place, cover the bottom of the pot with a layer of sifted compost mix.

Procedure for making wire staples to fix screening mesh

1. Cut a length of wire appropriate for the size of the hole and wrap it once around a cylindrical object such as a pencil or a marking pen.

2. Slip the object out of the coil and repeat the process slightly further along the wire so that you have two loops.

3. Bend the ends of the wire downwards.

4. Push the ends through a suitable piece of screening mesh.

5. Push the ends through the drainage hole and flatten them out on the underside of the pot.

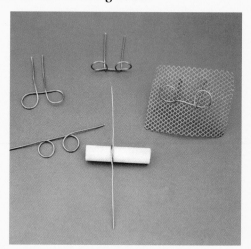

Procedure for fixing screening mesh and retaining wire when there is only one drainage hole

1. Cut a piece of strong wire slightly longer than the diameter of the drainage hole.

2. Wind a length of thinner wire around the piece of strong wire.

3. Push the wires through the drainage hole.

4. Slide a piece of screening mesh down over the drainage hole.

5. The stronger wire will sit across the bottom of the hole and hold the thinner wire in place, preventing it from being pulled up through the hole on tightening. The thinner wire will prevent the drainage mesh from slipping out of place and can be used to hold the tree in the pot.

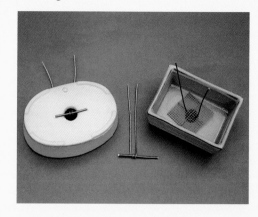

Removing the Tree from the Pot

Cut through any retaining wires that are still in place and loosen the wires on the screening mesh before you start to remove the tree from its original pot. If the existing pot is of the cascade type, or if it has an incurving rim, it may be difficult to remove the tree from it. Do not try to get the tree out by pulling on the trunk. Gently ease the tree out by using a root hook as a lever, making sure that you do not damage the pot. Pushing a piece of wooden dowelling up through one of the drainage holes can help to dislodge the tree. Do not worry if the outer roots are damaged – sometimes this is unavoidable, and they will be cut off when you start pruning the roots anyway.

Inspecting the Rootball

When the tree has been removed from the pot, inspect its roots thoroughly. You should be looking for any root rot, or pests such as vine weevils and leather jackets in the soil, as well as ascertaining whether the soil is of the correct mix. This is also a good time to look at the flare of the tree's roots and to assess ways in which this might be improved.

When a healthy pine or oak is taken from its pot a white mycorrhyzal fungus (*mycelium*) will most likely be present. It looks alarming but it is in fact highly beneficial to the health of the tree. The relationship between the trees and the fungus is symbiotic – one is dependent on the other. Mycelium attaches itself to the root system and enhances its efficiency in absorbing moisture and nutrients from the soil. If possible, it should be saved, crumbled and mixed with the new compost to encourage it to grow again.

Root rot is evidence of poor drainage. This may have been caused by blockage of the drainage holes or because of too much fine dust and not enough coarse material in the soil mix. If the soil mix has been at fault, make sure that the new soil mix is of a more gritty structure and that any fine dust is sifted out.

If you find a host of grubby lodgers, deal with them in the required manner (*see* Chapter 9), and ensure that all signs of infestation are eradicated. They will attack the tree's roots and, like all unwanted guests, eat it out of house and home. Other lodgers, in the form of weeds, may also have taken up residence in the pot. The pine seedling pictured (*see* page 90) is self-seeded from a garden tree and is taking up space and nourishment that was intended for the pot's original tenant. A weed is simply a plant growing where it is not wanted, so the pine has become a weed and should be removed. (This particular seedling was potted up and used in the landscape planting shown in Chapter 15.)

Tree in tall narrow pot: trees growing in incurving or cascade type pots can be difficult to remove. More frequent re-potting may be advisable when using these types of pots

Mycelium on roots of a mountain pine: the fungus and tree are symbiotic and the fungus helps to keep the tree healthy

Pine lodger: this pine seedling, although harmless now, will soon become a pest and should be removed

Re-potting gives the opportunity to eliminate persistent weeds. Some of these seem almost impossible to eradicate by means other than patient tracing and removal of their roots. Do not be tempted to use a selective weedkiller on persistent weeds. It will break down when it touches garden soil, but garden soil has a very different composition from bonsai soil, and the weedkiller may elect to kill the tree instead of the weeds.

If the tree's roots have been growing in a spiral around the sides of the pot, leaving the middle of the pot devoid of roots, there must be a reason for it. Perhaps the roots were not cut back hard enough when the tree was last re-potted, and just carried on growing as they had done before. However, it could also denote something more serious, such as bad watering or inhospitable soil. Steps need to be taken to regenerate roots nearer to the trunk of the tree. Carefully scrape away *all* of the soil in the affected area, so that it can be replaced with a more suitable mix and, if possible, cut back some of the heavier roots to encourage new root growth. If the soil is too compacted to scrape away without damaging the tree, soak the root-ball in water for a few hours and use a hose with a jet nozzle attachment to wash the soil away slowly.

Look at the distribution of the roots and the way in which they have grown. They should flare evenly from the trunk. If they do not, encourage root formation in blank areas and arrange the existing roots in a manner that is more visually pleasing. Try to uncross any roots that have grown over each other and spread the other roots out.

If ugly surface lumps and humps have formed in the roots, and there is enough root growth elsewhere to support the tree, cut the lumps out, remembering to protect all cut areas with wound sealant. Do not try and wire roots in place; they will resent it, as their cell structure differs from that of branches and is far more susceptible to damage. Weight or wedge them down instead.

Correct as many faults as you can but never put the tree in danger purely for aesthetic reasons. Other opportunities for improvement will arise when the tree has to be re-potted again in a few years' time.

Root-Pruning

When the tree is first taken out of its pot there is likely to be a solid mass of root, which will need to be reduced by approximately one-third before re-potting. Untangle the rootball, teasing out those long roots that have curled themselves around the side of the pot. If the tree is small this might be accomplished with the use of a chopstick; if the tree is large, a root hook and quite a lot of force may be needed. These long roots are now useless and can be cut off. Do not worry at this stage whether the cuts should be made on the slant or straight across; just make sure that the scissors or shears you use are very sharp – a clean cut will not leave jagged root edges that would be prone to rot. Cleanliness of the cut is far more important than the angle at which the cut is made.

If you measure the tree up against the pot at this stage, even after removing much of the root, you will wonder how the tree survived in such cramped conditions.

Any thick roots that are not serving as surface roots should be cut back. As they disappear below soil level, thick surface roots should get finer and finer. If there are large cuts on any roots, seal the wounds with a sealant. If the tree was growing in the ground the taproot would be necessary to stop the tree from falling over. Wires will now serve this purpose, holding the tree firmly in the pot, so the taproot is no longer required. Cut it back as far as you can.

Try to cut all feeding roots back to a growing rootlet that will take over from the one you have cut off. Just as you would not normally leave a branch completely bare of shoots when you prune it, so you should not leave a root completely bare of rootlets to continue feeding the tree.

If the root mass is so dense that it is impossible to separate the roots, loosen those roots that you can, then cut around the rootball with a pair of sharp shears. Then cut wedge shapes into the remaining rootball so that fresh compost can be worked between the old roots. Keep a note of which areas have been cut away so that a different area can be cut into the next time that the tree is re-potted. In this way, all of the compost will eventually be replaced, allowing fresh roots to grow throughout the whole root system.

The rootball does not have to be evenly pruned. It may be necessary to cut more roots off one side than another, in order to reposition the tree in its pot. In all, the rootball should

be reduced in size by about one-third. However, pines have a scant root system and care must be taken not to cut the roots back too hard. When the root-pruning is complete, there should be space all around the edge of the pot, to allow the tree to carry on growing. The tree will still be pot-bound but there will be enough room for the new roots to develop into a fine feeding system.

Always try to keep tree and root in proportion. If you have severely reduced the root system, you may need to prune the tree correspondingly. Until you are experienced in re-potting that particular tree and know how it reacts, err on the side of caution and maintain slightly more root than branch.

If at any time during the root-pruning process the roots look as though they are drying out, spray them immediately. To be on the safe side, spray the roots regularly anyway. If you are not accustomed to re-potting trees, the process may take longer than anticipated and the tree could suffer. Adding a small

Equipment checklist: potting and re-potting bonsai trees		
Ideal	**Emergency alternative**	**Purpose**
Ceramic or terracotta bonsai pot	Plastic pot or seed tray	In which to pot or re-pot the tree
Screening mesh	Plastic greenhouse shading mesh	To cover drainage holes in pots
Wire		To secure screening mesh and to secure tree in pot
Wire cutters and pliers		To cut wire to length and tighten retaining wires
Pre-sieved soil mixed to suit tree and conditions	Loam-based potting compost	In which to plant the tree
Large plastic bag	Carrier bag	To cover the tree's roots if the re-potting process is delayed
Spray bottle (full of water)	Recycled household spray (full of water)	To keep roots moist at all times
Large root cutters	Secateurs	To cut back heavy roots and taproots
Small root cutters	Scissors	To cut back fine roots
Chopsticks	Knitting needles	To tease out fine roots and work soil into the roots
Soil scoop	Flour scoop	Distributing soil in the pot
Root hook	Large kitchen fork with bent tines	To untangle the rootball
Turntable	TV stand or cake-icing stand	To gain easy access to all points without having to pick up the pot
Brush	Small paintbrush or make-up brush	To smooth surface of soil
Pieces of moss		To enhance display

amount of hormone rooting agent to the spray may help the roots recover more quickly, especially on trees that have a poor root system or are still in training and have very few fine feeding roots.

Planting the Tree in its Pot

Placement

When the root-pruning has been completed, the aesthetics of bonsai design come into play again. The tree needs to be placed in the pot in the best possible position and at the best height to enhance the tree's visual aspects. Choose a position that shows off the tree's trunk line and root flare to its best advantage.

Do not plant the tree in the middle or at the front of the pot. The tree should only be planted centrally if the pot is round. Mentally divide the pot into quarters and plant the tree off-centre in either of the back two sections. The tree should be tilted forward slightly to give a more natural impression and should not be planted so deeply that its roots are totally hidden.

Try the tree in various positions before you decide which is best, then squat down and view it at eye level, just to double-check your judgement, before wiring it in the pot.

Planting

When you are satisfied with the positioning of the tree, make sure that there is sufficient compost under it to eliminate any air pockets and then wire it into place. It should be held firmly. If the tree moves in the wind, the smallest of its newly growing root hairs may be damaged. If you can rock it backwards or forwards even slightly, the retaining wires need to be further tightened. Use a pair of pliers to twist the wires tighter if necessary, taking care not to damage the roots. This may seem an unnecessary chore as the tree will become firm in the pot as soon as its roots grow again. However, before this happens the tree is just too susceptible to damage to be left to its own devices. If it should fall over with its roots exposed for any length of time, you will have wasted all that effort and, more importantly, the tree may die.

When the tree is firmly fixed, pour small amounts of compost over its roots, carefully working it down into the pot with a chopstick or knitting needle. Rotate the chopstick to ensure that compost fills up every little cavity. The final level of the compost should be about one-fifth of an inch (half a centimetre) below the rim of the pot so that water will not run off the edge of the pot before it can soak into the compost.

Finishing Touches

Add moss to the surface to make it look more natural, remembering that the moss is there to give the impression of a cool green area at the base of the tree, and should not cover the whole surface of the compost. Blackbirds are notorious moss-removers; pinning moss down with small pieces of bent wire might make it slightly more difficult for birds to pull it up.

Accent plantings will also need re-potting, so keep an eye on them too

Procedure for re-potting trees

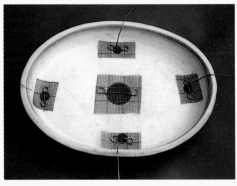

1. Prepare the pot by washing it to ensure that no diseases are passed on, then put drainage screening mesh and retaining wires in place.

2. Cover the bottom of the pot with a layer of potting compost.

3. Remove the tree from its pot, first cutting and removing any retaining wires, then inspect the root-ball for pests and root rot.

4. Tease out excessive growth with a root hook or chopstick and cut it off with sharp scissors.

5. Cut back any thick roots to a side rootlet that will take over its function.

6. The remaining rootball should be about one-third smaller than it was.

7. Ugly roots can be eliminated progressively each time the tree is re-potted.

Procedure for re-potting trees *continued*

8. Place the tree in the pot at the desired angle, remembering that the tree should be placed in the rear section of the pot.

10. Water the tree thoroughly with a fine rose, or mist-spray, and place in a protected position. *Do not water the tree again until it is almost dry.*

9. Wire the tree in place to prevent it falling from the pot, then add compost, carefully working it around the roots. Ensure that there are no large air pockets that might harm the roots. Place moss around the tree to enhance its appearance.

Now is the time to use your peat and clay siftings. Mould the mixture into a flat pancake and place it on the top of the compost to form an even base for the moss to grow into. Alternatively, sprinkle crushed-up particles of dried moss on to the surface of the compost. With luck, the spores will quickly produce an attractive fine green layer on top of the soil.

Carefully brush the surface of the compost to level it and remove any unwanted particles of moss. Water the tree thoroughly, taking care not to disturb the compost, then mist-spray the whole tree and stand it in a protected area.

Aftercare

Stressed trees are vulnerable and should be protected not only from frost but also from heat, wind and excessive watering. Water the tree carefully and thoroughly immediately after re-potting and then leave it until the soil is almost dry before watering it again. Do not keep pouring water on it – excessive watering causes pruning wounds to rot. As you've already cut away the unwanted roots, any further root loss could have disastrous results.

Newly re-potted trees should not be fed for several weeks. The developing roots are very fragile and easily damaged by strong fertilizers. Also, feeding before the leaves have opened could cause growth that the reduced root system cannot sustain. Wait until the leaves have opened and then feed them in the normal way (*see* fertilizers in Chapter 6).

If water sits on the top of the compost, it indicates that something has gone wrong in the re-potting process. The compost mix may not have had enough coarse material in it or it may have been tamped down too hard in the pot. To ensure a healthy tree, there is no alternative other than to repeat the process, correcting any errors that may have been made.

Afterthought – Accent Plantings

Don't forget to re-pot the accent plantings, as they quickly become pot-bound too. Ordinary potting compost is an acceptable planting medium but the spent compost from your trees is perfectly all right as long as it is free from grubs and the tree that was growing in it was healthy.

9 Pests, Diseases and Hygiene

General Principles

A pest is any creature or insect that causes damage to your tree; a disease is a pathological condition caused by a fungus, bacterium or a virus; and a disorder is caused by a nutritional deficiency or by inhospitable growing conditions. Bonsai trees are susceptible to all of them, although some species of tree are more prone to attacks than others. As the trees are likely to be displayed in close proximity, it usually happens that if one specimen of a species gets it, then all the others of that species will get it too.

You should be aware that, sometimes, trees just die for no apparent reason, of no obvious disease. It is a distressing fact but one that has to be accepted.

Eventually you will get to know how your tree looks on a day-to-day basis and will notice quickly if it is ailing in some way. Problems occur more frequently in the summer than in the winter but wilt, curled leaves, sticky surfaces, yellowing or browning foliage, spots, distorted growth and general lack of vigour can attack any tree at any time. There is usually a culprit lurking somewhere. The trick is to tackle a problem early enough, in order to stop a minor attack becoming a full infestation or an epidemic.

If possible, try to solve pest problems by non-chemical methods such as manual removal or washing off with a water spray. Only if this proves ineffective should you resort to chemical treatments. Biological methods are useful in the confined conditions of a greenhouse but outside in the open air they are, in most cases, less effective. Some plants react badly to chemicals and, although a list of such plants is usually given with the instructions for use, it cannot always be complete. Before trying a new chemical on your favourite tree try it on another, less important tree of the same species. If it is effective in controlling the problem and causes no adverse side effects, you can use it generally.

Some advice about the use of chemicals on bonsai trees advocates that, as bonsai trees are small, any chemicals should be used in diluted form. This is nonsense and, indeed, positively harmful. Always use chemicals strictly according to the manufacturer's instructions; diluted insecticides and fungicides just make problems more resistant to control, meaning that stronger chemicals eventually need to be used. If they are too concentrated they are no more effective; they kill the tree as well as the problem. Never use herbicides of any description near your trees. Selective weedkillers may be effective in your garden but in your pots they will kill the trees as well as the weeds that surround them.

There are far too many pests and diseases that affect different species and varieties of tree for them all to explained in one section of a book. For further advice on pests or diseases, consult a good gardening manual or specialist book on gardening problems. Specific brands or types of insecticide or fungicide have not been recommended here; there are so many on the market, and new improved products are constantly being introduced.

TOP RIGHT: Chafer larvae are root-feeding and should be picked out and destroyed when found

Pests

Aphids, Blackfly and Greenfly

Before noticing aphids on your trees, you might see a parade of ants walking up and down shepherding aphid herds. Greenfly and blackfly all leave a sticky substance behind them, which not only clogs the pores of leaves but also makes them prone to a black sooty mould. Also, aphids can distort foliage and pass on plant viruses.

Aphids do not actually chew on a leaf; they simply pierce it and let the pressure within the plant push food into their mouths. No matter how many predators there are – in the shape of ladybirds – the aphid population always seems to be one step ahead. Aphids are born with embryonic aphids already growing inside them.

If there are only a few aphids present they can be picked off or crushed with the fingers. If they become a problem, a few squirts with soapy water or a gentle natural insecticide will usually get rid of them.

Birds

On limes, gall mites cause red spikes (BOTTOM); on elms they cause pimples (TOP)

Birds are generally welcome in the garden and the tiny wrens that nip about bonsai trees lifting off insects are a positive boon. Mistle thrushes lift off the snails and smash them on convenient stones but their near relatives, blackbirds, pull up all the moss around the trees and then dig holes and tug hard on the roots as though they were worms. To discourage blackbirds, cover the compost with loosely woven greenhouse shading and pin it in place with a bit of wire. It is not 100 per cent effective but is far better than watching in frustration as another bird comes along and lifts the moss that you have just replaced.

Caterpillars

Caterpillars are the larvae of moths and butterflies and are very selective in what they eat, often being plant-specific. Damaged leaves are evidence of their presence. Inspect the tree thoroughly and pick off any offenders.

Chafer Larvae

Chafer larvae are creamy-white, root-feeding grubs with curved bodies, brown heads and three pairs of legs. They are the larvae of beetles such as the cockchafers and garden chafers. Usually they are not a chronic problem in bonsai trees and can simply be picked out and destroyed when seen at re-potting time.

Gall Mites

Elm, lime, hawthorn, beech and maple are among the species that are affected by gall mites. The way in which they make their presence felt differs from tree to tree and the type of mite that is causing the damage. On limes, the mite causes red spikes to grow from the leaf; on elms, you might see light-coloured pimples; on maples, it causes white hairs on the underside of the leaves. The galls are disfiguring but seldom lead to the demise of the tree. If possible, remove the affected leaves and spray with an insecticide to prevent further attacks.

Pets

Household pets are not generally thought of as pests, but a dog urinating on a tree will do immense harm. Place the tree on benching or on a stand to keep it out of harm's way.

Red Spider Mites

When conditions are dryer than usual, red spider mites can be found on pines, junipers, firs and elms. Their fine webs are fairly easily spotted but to be sure that it is not a simple spider in residence place a piece of white paper below the affected branch and shake it lightly. Red spider mites will appear on the paper as tiny pepper-like dots. They affect some parts of the tree more than others and cause foliage to yellow, with a fine mottling occurring before the leaves fall off.

The most effective control of red spider mite is to keep the leaves well sprayed with water. Should the tree become infested, spray with a proprietary soap-based insecticide solution. Red spider is one pest that is becoming increasingly resistant to insecticide control, so prevention is better than cure. Mist-spray the underside of the tree's leaves on a regular basis to increase humidity and deter the mites from taking up residence in your trees.

Rose Leaf-Rolling Sawfly

Technically, this bug should attack only roses but it has been known to affect ash, too. The sides of the leaflets are rolled into a tight tube

TOP RIGHT: *The ends of leaflets can be curled into tight rolls in which insects live*

during the spring and early summer. The female sawfly secretes a chemical when she lays her eggs and it is this that causes the leaf to roll. Pale green caterpillar-like insects feed inside the leaflets. Pull off the leaves and destroy them, or spray with a systemic insecticide.

Scale Insects

Maple, pyracantha and cotoneaster are frequently attacked by the larger type of scale insect while junipers are prone to attacks from the tiny ones, which resemble a dusting of dandruff. The former is much easier to spot and to deal with than the latter.

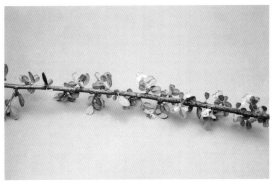

Scale insects can be difficult to spot on brown bark but they are there as round raised bumps on the underside of this cotoneaster twig. The minute white scale insects that can infest junipers are a major problem

Both slugs and snails can be a problem in soft-leafed trees and can reduce leaves to lace curtains overnight

The larger type of scale insect is to be found glued limpet-like to the trunk and branches of trees. They can be more difficult to spot on old bark than on newer green wood, but are easily dislodged with the fingers. After removal they leave a discoloured circle, which should be cleaned to avoid fungus infections.

The white scale insects that attack junipers are smaller than a pinhead and can cause the total demise of the tree before they are discovered. The insects lodge in the scales of the juniper and multiply at an alarming rate. There is no possibility of dislodging them by hand and, as normal insecticides will not penetrate their hard shell, systemic insecticides are at present the best way of eliminating them.

Vine-weevil grubs can do immense damage to accent plantings and to the softer roots of trees

Slugs and Snails

Prickly trees are not really susceptible to attacks from slugs and snails but soft-leafed trees are, especially in the spring when the leaves are emerging and at their most appetizing. For some reason, both slugs and snails are particularly attracted to laburnum and can turn its leaves into lace curtains in a night. Eliminate the problem by regularly checking under the pots and around the benching to see if any slugs or snails are hiding there. If they cannot be located, a few slug pellets placed at the base of the tree will soon solve the problem.

Vine Weevils

Problems with vine weevils are twofold: the adult beetles eat the leaves of trees and the larvae eat the roots. The adult beetle, which is grey and about half an inch (1cm) long with a pointed nose, does not do a great deal of damage to established trees, just notching the edges of leaves and making them unsightly. However, its greedy offspring can do untold damage if left unchecked.

The first sign of vine-weevil infestation may show up in soft-rooted accent plantings, which will suddenly wilt and fall over. Investigation may reveal a crowd of fat curved white grubs with brown snouts munching through everything in sight. Eradication is not easy and until recently the only method of control was through the biological use of nematodes, which attacked and killed the grubs. However, new, more effective products against vine weevils are now available from most good garden centres.

Fortunately, the adult beetles cannot fly and cannot reach trees if easy access is denied. Keep trees off the ground and place the legs of any stands into a tin or saucer of water, to make it even more difficult for the adults to get to the trees. The adult weevils have a clever survival trick of playing dead when disturbed. Don't be fooled; take measures to ensure that they really are dead.

Whitefly

Whiteflies are exactly as their name suggests – small flies with white wings. The signs of whitefly infestation are similar to those of aphid attack: a sticky coating that appears on the leaves is in fact whitefly excrement. Under cover, whitefly can be biologically controlled through the use of a parasitic wasp but this is impractical in an outdoor environment, where other methods of eradication have to be employed. Most insecticides will kill off whitefly and the use of a systemic insecticide may help to prevent further attacks.

Wood Lice

Wood lice (also known as slaters or pill bugs) are small, grey, segmented creatures that roll into a ball when disturbed. They are more or less harmless to your trees, living mainly on old leaves and other plant debris. Using screening mesh when potting up trees (*see* Chapter 8) will prevent them from setting up home in the base of the pots, and general hygiene will make the area less attractive to them.

Woolly Aphids

Woolly aphids are partial to pines and are easily spotted by the white fluffy deposits under which they live. They leave behind them the same sort of sticky substance that is left by other aphids, which encourages sooty mould and other funguses to take hold. Because soapy water does not penetrate the woolly coating of the aphid, it is necessary to kill these aphids through their diet, using a systemic insecticide that is absorbed by the tree.

Diseases

Azalea Gall

Fleshy pale green swellings appear on leaves, that later turn white before drying and turning black. Azalea gall is a fungus-born disease that can be difficult to eliminate totally but usually affects only a few leaves on the shrub. Pick off the affected leaves; if the problem is persistent, spray with a fungicide.

Coral Spot

Coral spot can affect maples, elms and beeches. Coral-coloured spots appear on the branches, then die back. Until fairly recently, coral spot only affected deadwood, and would not, therefore, have been a real problem in bonsai trees, but it is now becoming more aggressive and has

LEFT: Woolly aphids live under a white 'woolly' substance and are partial to pines

Azalea galls start as green swellings, then turn white before going black

started to attack live wood. Cut out and burn any affected branches. Clean pruning tools thoroughly as the fungus can spread from one tree to another through poor hygiene.

Black Spot

Black spot usually affects roses but can also attack elms. It is not very tolerant of air pollution and is more prevalent in areas of clean air. Black spots appear on leaves, which then turn yellow and fall off the tree. Treat the problem with a fungicide.

Mildew

Powdery mildew can affect trees and shrubs in damp humid weather. Leaves become coated with a white powdery substance, which can later turn to purple patches before the leaf yellows and falls off. It is caused by a variety of fungi and, surprisingly, it affects plants that have been growing in dry sites more than those that are in damp ones. To clear it, use a suitable fungicide, revise your watering regime and improve the air circulation around the tree.

Peach Leaf Curl

Peach leaf curl, caused by a fungus that is encouraged by cool wet conditions, can affect *prunus* varieties. The leaves become blistered and distorted and can later turn a deep red. Pick off the affected leaves and protect the tree. To prevent re-attack from over-wintering spores, spray the tree with a copper fungicide in mid-

to late winter.

Rust

If small bright orange or brown patches appear on the underside of leaves, with a corresponding yellow patch on the upper surface, the tree has rust, which can lead to early leaf fall. The disease is caused by a fungus and increases with high humidity. Remove affected material if possible and, as the spores can over-winter on the tree, spray it with a suitable fungicide and improve the air circulation around the tree.

Scab

Scab is a fungus-spread disease that thrives in damp weather and manifests itself with scabby dark patches on leaves and fruit. It can affect pyracantha as well as apples. Cut off affected material, spray with a suitable fungicide and improve air circulation around the plant.

Sooty Mould

This black mould, which affects pines and other trees, forms on the sticky substance (insect excreta) left by aphids or whitefly. Apply an insecticide to kill the aphids and a fungicide to clear the mould. A soapy solution might solve both problems.

Mildew causes white marks on leaves and many trees are susceptible to attack in humid weather conditions

Witches' Broom

A witches' broom is a bundle of distorted twigs that grows broom-like on birches and horn-beams. It is caused by an attack of mites or by a fungus. If any of your trees are affected in this way simply cut off the affected part and destroy it.

Physiological Disorders

Chlorosis

Chlorosis displays itself in azaleas and acid-loving trees by yellowing of the leaves and is generally caused by lack of iron. Treat the tree to a dose of sequestered iron and consider changing the compost mix when next re-potting.

Die-Back

There can be several causes for die-back, many of which point to root problems, but it can also be caused simply by lack of light. Foliage needs light to do its job, without light the foliage does not function properly and the tree will discard it. The problem can be alleviated by reposi-tioning the tree or remembering to turn it reg-ularly to ensure that all sides have adequately sunlight.

Drought

Trees can recover quite well from drought if it is not prolonged. The symptoms of drought are wilting and dried leaves, and early autumn colour. Do not discard the tree even if all of its leaves have fallen off. If the compost has a high peat content, watering with a spray will not be sufficient. Soak the tree thoroughly by placing it in a bowl of water up to the rim of the pot for half an hour. Do not leave it with its feet in water in the long term, as this will just cause other problems.

Nitrogen Deficiency

High-nitrogen fertilizers are usually discouraged in the growing of bonsai and this can some-times lead to nitrogen deficiency, which mani-fests itself in pale yellow foliage and spindly growth. A good feed of blood, fish and bone will usually sort out the problem. Alternatively, an application of a soluble garden fertilizer will provide a short-term solution to the problem.

Root Rot

Root rot can lead to die-back in the branches of the tree as well as the roots and ultimately can lead to the death of the tree. The cause is usually over-watering but could also be due to the use of an inappropriate compost mix (*see* Chapter 8).

RIGHT: Witches' broom is a bundle of distorted twigs, caused by an attack from a fungus or a mite

LEFT: Sooty mould forms on the sticky substance left behind by aphids and other insects

Lack of light can cause die-back of foliage

RIGHT: *Should lichens be removed or allowed to grow?*

The alpines in this pot have now reached 'weed' status and will have to be manually removed. Even a wild strawberry has taken up residence

Weeds

Bonsai pots are full of healthy compost, which provide ideal growing conditions for weeds as well as trees. Remove the weeds as soon as they are spotted as they will take up food and moisture meant for the tree. Never be tempted to treat persistent weeds with weedkillers; carefully remove all of their roots with tweezers when you next re-pot.

Wilt

Wilts can have a number of causes. First, check that the compost is not overly dry and that the wilt has not been caused by drought conditions. If the compost is moist, then there may be problems with the roots. If possible, lift the tree to check that the roots are healthy. If they are, the cause is likely to come from a virus attack of some description which, unfortunately, may mean disposing of the tree.

Basic Hygiene

Keeping trees clean, as well as fertilized, is one of the best aids to keeping them healthy and discouraging pests. Remove weeds and clear away dead or diseased leaves. Never recycle compost from a tree that has died from a known or unknown cause.

There is some debate over whether or not to leave lichens on trees. Dying branches of larch and pine are usually completely covered in those grey lichens that are commonly found on deadwood in forest trees. Is the lichen there because the branch is dying, or is the branch dying because it is covered in lichen? Bark needs to breathe, so it should be kept clean and not clogged up with mosses, lichens or any other substances. Removing these grey lichens is a good idea, although you could leave a small patch if you prefer. Lichens are easily removed with the fingers or with light brushing with a toothbrush. Trees with clean trunks and branches grow and thicken much more rapidly than those that cannot breathe freely.

The orange and yellow lichens that frequently appear do not seem to cause so much of a problem, as they are highly decorative and slow-growing.

Algae have grown on this juniper during the winter months and have totally obscured the bark's colour. A couple of minutes' work with a toothbrush will reveal the beautiful red-brown bark

During the winter months, both the trunks and branches of your trees will probably acquire a film of green algae, which you may or may not find visually pleasing. Resist the temptation to leave it on the tree as this also clogs up the bark and stops it breathing, seriously curtailing its growth. The colour of the bark is hidden under the algae and should be revealed. The only tools needed to restore the bark's colour, health and vigour are a toothbrush, a mug of water and some patience. A special brass-headed brush, which has a polishing effect on the bark, is available, but a toothbrush will do job almost as well.

Unless the tree has had an attack from aphid or other pests during the summer, and you think that they may still be lurking in the bark ready to pounce again, do not add a detergent to the cleaning water. However, if you are in doubt, add a couple of drops of washing-up liquid to the water and then rinse it off thoroughly. You will be surprised at how much algae is removed and how many times the water needs to be changed. You will also be surprised at the improvement in the growth rate of the tree.

In evergreens, the foliage as well as the trunks and branches will become covered in algae. Although it is not as evident on scales or needles as it is on bark, it is there and should be removed. Using a toothbrush and clean water, gently brush the foliage pad a few times to remove the green film.

III
Creating the Tree

10 Material Suitable for Bonsai Training

General Principles

Bonsai are created from normal species of trees, not from their specially dwarfed varieties, and as there are upwards of 60,000 different species of tree in existence, the list of those suitable for bonsai training is almost endless. The trees listed here are simply those that are the most readily available and the easiest to propagate.

Before choosing a tree to work on, think about the climactic conditions in your locality. There is no point in making the task more difficult than it has to be. Baobabs grow well in Africa but they would not grow well in Norway. If the tree appears in your local garden centre, or there is a version growing in a nearby park, then it will be suitable to grow in a pot in your garden. If the tree is inside the greenhouse section of the garden centre, it will almost invariably be an indoor tree and should be treated accordingly.

If you wish to style a tree in a particular form, you may have to look at many trees before a suitable candidate for training is found. However, if you wish to train a particular species of tree, decide on a style that will suit the way the tree of your choice is growing. Do not try and force the tree into a style in which it would not naturally grow.

For ease of identification, trees have been listed under their common names under the following headings (regardless of whether the trees are deciduous or evergreen):

- broadleaf;
- conifers;
- flowering/fruiting; and
- indoor trees.

Birch

Broadleaf Evergreen and Deciduous Trees and Shrubs

Alder	*Alnus glutinosa*
Ash	*Fraximus excelsior*
Beech	
Common Beech	*Fagus sylvatica*
Copper Beech	*Fagus sylvatica 'Purpurea'*
Japanese White Beech	*Fagus crenata*
Birch	
Downy Birch	*Betula pubescens*
Silver Birch	*Betula pendula*
Box	*Buxus semperivens*
Dogwood	*Cornus sanguinea*
Elm	
Chinese Elm	*Ulmus parvifolia*
English Elm	*Ulmus procera*
Japanese Elm	*Zelkova serrata*
Hazel	
Corkscrew Hazel	*Corylus avellana 'Contorta'*
Nut Hazel	*Corylus avellana*
Honeysuckle	*Lonicera morowanii*
Hornbeam	*Carpinus betulus*
Judas Tree	*Cercis siliquastrum*
Lime	*Tilia cordata*
Locust	*Robinia pseudoacacia*
Maple	
Amur Maple	*Acer ginnala*
Butterfly Maple	*Acer palmatum 'Butterfly'*
Cork Bark Maple	*Acer palmatum 'Nishiki Gawa'*
Cut-Leaf Maple	*Acer palmatum 'Dissectum'*
Field Maple	*Acer campestre*
Japanese Maple	*Acer palmatum*
Paper Bark Maple	*Acer griseum*
Trident Maple	*Acer buergerianum*
Oak	
English Oak	*Quercus robur*
Holm Oak	*Quercus ilex*
Poplar	
White Poplar	*Populus alba*
Black Poplar	*Populus nigra*
Lombardy Poplar	*Populus nigra 'Italica'*
Privet	*Ligistrum lucidum*
Rowan	*Sorbus aucuparia*

Hazel

Box

Lime

Atlantic Cedar

Stewartia   *Stewartia monodelpha*
Sweet Gum   *Liquidambar*
                     styraciflua

Sycamore   *Acer pseudoplatanus*
Willow
     Crack Willow   *Salix fragailis*
     Weeping Willow   *Salix sepulcralis*

Coniferous Trees

Cedar
     Atlas Cedar   *Cedrus atlantica*
     Cedar of Lebanon   *Cedrus libani*
     Cedar Deodar   *Cedrus deodara*
     Japanese Cedar   *Cryptomeria japonica*
     Western Red Cedar   *Thuja plicata*
Cypress
     Hinoki Cypress   *Chamaecyparis obtusa*
     Sarawa Cypress   *Chamaecyparis pisifera*
     Swamp Cypress   *Taxodium distichum*
Fir
     Douglas Fir   *Pseudotsuga menziesii*
     Korean Fir   *Abies koreana*
     Silver Fir   *Abies alba*
Hemlock
     Canadian/Eastern   *Tsuga canadensis*
        Hemlock
     Western Hemlock   *Tsuga heterophylla*
Juniper
     Nepal Juniper   *Juniperus squamata*
                     'Meyeri'
     Chinese Juniper   *Juniperus chinensis*
     Common Juniper   *Juniperus communis*
     Prostrate Juniper   *Juniperus procumbens*
     Temple Juniper   *Juniperus rigida*
Larch
     European Larch   *Larix decidua*
     Japanese Larch   *Larix kaempferi*
Maidenhair Tree   *Gingko biloba*
Pine
     Bristlecone Pine   *Pinus aristata*
     Corsican Pine   *Pinus nigra* var.
                     maritima
     Japanese Black Pine   *Pinus thunbergii*
     Japanese White Pine   *Pinus parviflora*
     Lodgepole Pine   *Pinus contorta*
     Mountain Pine   *Pinus mugo*
     Scots Pine   *Pinus sylvestris*
Redwood
     Dawn Redwood   *Metasequoia*
                     glyptostroboides
     Giant Redwood   *Sequoiadendron*
                     gigantium

Korean Fir

Mountain Pine

English Yew

Forsythia

Quince

Apple

Hazel Catkin

Redwood	*Sequoia semperivens*
Spruce	
Alberta Spruce	*Picea glauca*
Norway Spruce	*Picea abies*
Sitka Spruce	*Picea sitchensis*
Yew	
English Yew	*Taxus baccata*
Japanese Yew	*Taxus cuspidata*

Flowering/Fruiting Trees and Shrubs

Apricot	*Prunus mume*
Azalea	*Rhododendron indicum – Satsuki*
Barberry	*Berberis thunbergii*
Blackthorn	*Prunus spinosa*
Camellia	*Camellia*
Cherry	
Bird Cherry	*Prunus padus*
Japanese Flowering Cherry	*Prunus serrulata*
Cotoneaster	*Cotoneaster cashmiriensis microphyllus*
Crab Apple	*Malus floribunda*
Firethorn	*Pyracantha angustifolia*
Forsythia	*Forsythia intermedia*
Guelder Rose	*Viburnum opulus*
Hawthorn	*Crataegus oxycantha*
Holly	*Ilex aquifolium*
Jasmine	*Jasminium nudiflorum*
Laburnum	*Laburnum anagyroides*
Lilac	*Syringa*
Magnolia	*Magnolia*
Peach	*Prunus persica*
Pomegranate	*Punica granatum*
Potentilla	*Potentilla fruticosa*
Quince	
Common Quince	*Cydonia oblonga*
Japanese Quince	*Chaenomeles japonica*
Rhododendron	*Rhododendron*
Rowan	*Sorbus aucuparia*
Spiraea	*Spiraea japonica*
Tamarisk	*Tamarix parviflora*
Weigela	*Weigela florida*
Wisteria	
Chinese Wisteria	*Wisteria sinensis*
Japanese Wisteria	*Wisteria floribunda*

Indoor Trees

Bougainvillea

Azalea	*Rhododendron*
Bougainvillea	*Bougainvillea buttiana*
Fig	*Ficus benjamina*
Gardenia	*Gardenia jasminoides*
Hibiscus	*Hibiscus rosa-sinensis*
Jacaranda	*Jacaranda ovalifolia*
Jade Tree	*Crassula arborescens*
Podocarpus	*Podocarpus macrophyllus*
Sageretia	*Sageretia theezans*
Serissa	*Serissa foetida*

11 Pruning for Shape, *Jins* and *Sharis*

General Principles

The creation of a new bonsai tree, or the restyling of an existing one, is likely to entail major surgery involving the removal of branches. No patient would choose to undergo major surgery for anything other than a life-threatening condition unless they were fit for it. The same reasoning applies to trees. Do not prune them for styling unless they are healthy. Newly lifted trees can take a long time to recover their vigour, so do not rush in and style them before they are ready. Wait until the tree has a good root system or select another tree to work on.

Learn as much as you can about the growing habits of the tree before you start to prune it. Is it a species that buds back easily or one of those that has to have a growing tip? Study the line of the trunk and the flare of the roots to find a front and a back for the tree. Assess the position of the dominant branches, deciding which you want to retain and which ones you want to discard. Only when you are sure of your aims should you start to cut branches from the tree. Once you have made a decision, stick with it and get on with the job.

An alternative to the total removal of part of the tree is to use the equivalent of cosmetic surgery and turn a fault into a feature of interest by creating a *jin* or a *shari*. A *jin* is a branch, or area of a branch, that has been stripped of bark and retained as deadwood; a *shari* is an area of trunk that has undergone similar treatment. The terms are specific to parts of the tree: *jins* are always on branches, *sharis* are always on trunks.

If the roots of the tree have been cut back hard during re-potting, it is advisable also to prune the top of the tree so that a balance between root and foliage is formed. Likewise, if the top of the tree is heavily pruned, it might be necessary to cut back some roots to compensate for the lack of foliage. If the tree is vigorous and growing well, removing a lot of branches will leave it with excessive energy, which may result in rosettes of buds appearing around every cut. If back-budding is desired in

Japanese Flowering Cherry: deciduous trees can often be hard-pruned to encourage the development of new branches

110

the tree, this is the ideal way to induce it. Unwanted buds can be rubbed off with the thumb or trimmed off in the spring.

Why Prune?

In an existing tree, summer pruning will have maintained its basic shape but there will come a time when upper branches become too thick or the tree becomes too tall, and harsher pruning is called for. Young trees have a mass of thin branches, whereas mature trees have fewer but heavier branches. When developing a bonsai from a young tree it is necessary to remove some of these branches if the illusion of age is to be achieved.

Pruning is carried out for several reasons:

- to keep the tree small enough to to fit in a particular pot;
- to shape and style the tree;
- to promote the growth of new buds and renew the tree's vigour;
- to remove or disguise ugly features;
- to create *jins* and *sharis* for interest;
- to create areas of negative space, to bring balance to the tree; and
- to enable air to circulate freely around the tree, thereby improving its health.

During the styling of new bonsai trees, pruning is required to clear the tree of unwanted growth and create 'space'. When you look up through the branches of a natural tree, you can see pieces of sky. A bonsai tree should have similar areas where it would theoretically be possible to see the sky. Often referred to as 'negative space', this part of the tree is devoid of growth and visually balances areas where growth is heavy. These spaces are an important part of the tree's visual development and also allow air to freely flow around the tree.

When To Prune

Pruning for shape is usually undertaken during the months when the tree is dormant. At this time, there is less sap rising and, consequently, less likelihood of the tree bleeding. On trees that do not bleed, such as maples, pruning can

Rule of thumb guide: pruning for shape	
Type of tree	**When to prune**
Deciduous	Spring to autumn
Conifers	Winter or very early spring
Flowering trees	Early spring or after flowering
Fruit trees	Autumn or early spring
Indoor bonsai	At almost any time
Mame trees	In early spring

be undertaken at any time. Care has to be taken with pines, which can bleed profusely.

What to Prune

Study the tree carefully before cutting off any branches. Look to see what the tree tends to do naturally. Which style does it suggest before any training? Does it have a natural lean or cascade? Look at photographs of trees of that style, remembering that photographs give a flat image and that the tree will need back branches to give it depth. As a trunk needs to taper, it may need shortening and a new leader creating. Full details of styling a tree from garden centre material are given in Chapter 15.

Make a pencil sketch of the existing branches and erase those that are not needed. In this way you can see the effect before you make the cut and can pencil them back in again. Cutting off the branch before assessing its effect is a bit too permanent.

When you have chosen your style, prune away any branches:

- that are growing straight up or straight down;
- that are opposite each other, forming a T-bar, or in a whorl;
- that cross over other branches;
- that obscure the trunk or interfere with other branches;
- that prevent light reaching other branches;
- that are out of scale with their position (upper branches that are too thick);
- that are no longer needed for trunk thickening;
- that spoil the line of the tree's triangular shape.

Japanese Flowering Quince: this tree is in its initial stages of training after being lifted; trunk detail of the same Japanese Quince (MIDDLE); a new leader has been created to form an apex (BELOW)

How to Prune

Removing a Branch

For small to medium-sized branches, knob-cutters are invaluable. They are sharp and give a concave cut, which, when callused over, remains flat and unobtrusive. If knob-cutters are not available, cut the branch with secateurs. Run your finger over the cut to feel if it is flat and cut any remaining protruding bits with sharp scissors or a knife. Alternatively, you may wish to leave a stub of the branch and *jin* it (*see* page 115).

For large branches, first shorten the branch to a manageable length, using a saw if necessary. Shortening the branch will also reduce its weight and lower the risk of it tearing back and damaging the trunk's bark when it is finally cut through. Cover all cuts with a wound-sealing compound to lessen the risk of disease entering the wound.

Mountain pine: whorls of branches can leave ugly lumps that need pruning (TOP). Cover all cuts with a wound-sealing compound (BOTTOM)

Making a New Leader

When the top of an existing bonsai tree becomes too heavy, or if a lifted tree has been shortened, it is necessary to make a new leader from which a new apex can be formed. If only a small part of the tree has to be removed the problem can be solved simply by wiring the uppermost remaining branch/shoot in an upward position, but where the treatment has been more drastic more thought is required.

The Japanese Quince pictured (*see* page 112) has been reduced in height from around 12ft to 2ft (3.6m to 60cm), which has resulted in a large scar and the need for an entire new top to the tree to develop. An angled cut has been made just above the branch that was chosen to be the new leader and the branch was temporarily wired to hold it in an upright position. Eventually, the scar will heal and the new leader will be encouraged to twig and form an apex.

Mountain Pine: buds have formed on the old wood of this pine following pruning

there is foliage from which new shoots could form before pruning the branch. Without any growth to support, the branch may die.

Shortening an Over-Long Branch

When shortening an over-long branch, try to cut it back to a side shoot that will take over as the growing point. Make pruning cuts to branches with the cutters beneath the branch where possible. This will give a better line to the branch and encourage buds to form at the sides of the branch rather than below it.

Pruning for Back-Budding

Maintenance pruning will have encouraged buds to form at leaf nodes near the cut but, because energy is still being directed towards the new wood at the end of the branch, it will not have encouraged buds to form further down the branch. To get buds to form on old wood, the tree's energy has to be redirected, which means cutting off the end of the branch. Deciduous trees bud back fairly well on old wood but with conifers it is not always so easy. Check again on the growing habits of the tree. If you are unsure about its propensity for budding, make sure that

New shoots on a pine: when shortening pine branches, cut back to a new shoot to take over as the growing point

Jins

Sometimes, whole branches will die back in the upper parts of a tree, or a branch will tear off in a storm or under its own weight, leaving a short piece of wood still attached to the tree. All this has come about because of the hardships the tree has suffered at the hands of nature. Young trees are upright and flexible and do not suffer in this way. Artificially inducing

Oak with the scars of its battles with nature: branches have been torn from this tree several times during its life. One has left a snag of wood behind as it fell

---

Equipment checklist: *jins* and *sharis*

Item	Alternative	Purpose
Pruning shears/scissors	Secateurs	To cut off unwanted bits of the branch
Jinning knife	Penknife	To ring-cut the bark
Jinning pliers	Pliers	To crush the bark and tear back the *jin*
Wire brush	Sandpaper	To finish off rough edges
Wound-sealing compound	Wound-sealing compound	To seal the edges of living bark
Lime sulphur	Lime sulphur	To whiten and preserve the *jin* or *shari*
Power tools, for *sharis* and hollow-trunk effects	Chisels	To cut into and carve the trunk

---

Procedure for creating a *jin* from a branch

NB: The procedure for creating large *jins* and small *jins* is the same, but tools of the appropriate size will be required.

1. Having selected an appropriate branch, cut through the bark all the way around the branch at the point where the branch joins the trunk.

2. Using pliers, gently crush the bark so that it becomes loose on the branch and is easy to remove.

3. Strip the branch of bark.
4. Put wound-sealing compound around the edges of the cut bark. Cut off the twigs that are too thin to *jin*.

5. When the wood has dried, treat it with lime sulphur.

Procedure for creating a *jin* from the stub of a branch

1. Cut the branch to a stub.

2. Cut through the bark all the way around the branch at the point where the branch meets the trunk.

3. Crush the branch gently with pliers to loosen the bark.

4. Carefully remove the bark.

5. Using the pliers, tear back the branch so that the edges look more natural.

6. Smooth the branch with a stiff brush or sandpaper. When the wood has dried, treat it with lime sulphur.

these marks of age in a tree will add to its illusion of maturity.

Before making a *jin* on a tree, make sure that it is appropriate. The deadwood should tell a story and be suggestive of the tree's tribulations.

Traditionally, *jins* are induced only in coniferous trees, even though in nature there is just as much deadwood in the upper branches of deciduous trees. A *jin* on a rugged juniper looks sublime; a *jin* on a graceful maple is

San Jose Juniper on an artificial slab: this juniper had become overgrown and had lost its windswept shape (TOP). Instead of pruning, the branches have been jinned to add interest to the tree (BOTTOM). The tree was styled from garden-centre material and has been on the slab for eight years

TOP RIGHT: Collected omono-size yew after one year of training: this collected yew was probably about 100 years old before it was lifted but the addition of jins and sharis has given an ugly stump a grace and dynamism

incongruous. If a branch needs pruning from a deciduous tree do not *jin* it, bin it instead.

Shari and *Sabamiki*

The results from trees that have been given *sharis* and hollowed areas can be truly spectacular, but it is an advanced technique that needs to be carried out with great care if widespread die-back is to be avoided. Before achieving the creation of *sharis* and *sabamiki* (hollow-trunk) areas, it is very important to know the habits of the species of tree well before cutting deep into the trunk.

The tree must be in superb health before being treated in this way. The shock is immense and it can take a long time for the tree to recover. The yew pictured above was fed extensively and allowed to grow freely for three years after lifting before its training began. Initially, after the *shari* was made, most of the apex of the tree died back but, because the tree had such a strong root system, new growth quickly took its place.

Remember that deadwood really is dead, and will not regenerate and grow buds. Consequently, when choosing an area of trunk on which to cut a *shari*, care must be taken to ensure that it never encircles the tree, cutting off the lifeline from the tree's roots. Also, any branches above the *shari* are likely to die back if they are deprived of nutrients.

The *shari* should be confined to the trunk area and not extend below the surface of the compost, where rot would set into the cut area. Carefully mark out the area to be worked upon before cutting into the bark, using artistry to create a natural effect. Remember, natural deadwood seldom has straight edges.

Procedure for creating *sharis* and *sabamiki*

1. Mark out the area to treated with a water-soluble marker.
2. Cut around the area with a sharp knife.
3. Loosen the bark and strip it off.
4. Cover the edges of the bark with wound-sealing compound.
5. If a hollowed area (*sabamiki*) is to be included, re-mark the area to be treated.
6. Using the appropriate tools, cut into the trunk to the desired depth.
7. When the wood has dried out, treat it with lime sulphur.
8. Place the tree in a protected position.

---

12 Wiring to Shape

General Principles

Designing a tree might be an art but the process by which the design is achieved is a skill and, like all skills, needs to be practised. Seeing the wiring, the unitiated often believe that a bonsai tree is crippled, but this is not true. Correctly applied on a healthy tree, wire will not harm it, but will enhance the design beyond all expectations.

Character can often be pruned into deciduous trees but coniferous trees usually need extra help if they are to look more care-worn and noble. Wiring tends to produce curves rather than angles but, without wiring, your conifer may for ever look like a sapling. Simply checking the tree's upward surge by shortening its branches and bringing them downwards instantly makes the tree look older and the trunk thicker.

An analogy for the use of wiring is that of a broken limb, which is encased in plaster to ensure that the bone mends properly and straight. A plaster cast supplies a framework in which the limb can assume the desired shape so that it does not adopt any unwanted twists that would spoil its looks and restrict its use. If the cast is too tight, it will restrict the blood flow and the limb could be lost; if it is too loose, the limb could move about inside it causing the limb to distort and the skin to chafe.

The same principles apply to wiring a tree. Correct wiring will simply supply a basic framework into which a trunk or branch can grow, set and adopt the shape that you desire. You decide the shape of the framework, given the constraints of the branch and the species and design of the tree. If the wire is too tight on the branch, or is left on so long that the branch

Practise wiring on a branch from a garden shrub clamped in a bench vice

grows too big for it, the wire will cut deeply into the bark causing unsightly and unhealthy grooves. At best, the branch will be disfigured; at worst, it will be lost. If the wire is too loose, the desired shape will not be achieved, rubbing might damage the tree's bark, and the effort spent wiring will have been wasted.

Practise wiring on something that is unimportant to you – branches cut from garden hedges or bushes, for example. That *leylandii* hedge may be a visual irritant, but it can provide excellent twigs and branches of varying thickness on which you can practise your skills. Clamp the cut end in a work-bench vice to hold it steady, and wind away. If you start in this manner, you will soon be able to select the right type and thickness of wire and apply it to a tree

117

without damaging it or accidentally knocking off those precious side branches and buds.

Don't be tempted to rush the job and wire hastily. Slowly and gently is the way to proceed. Where bonsai trees are concerned, you always have time. Before you start wiring, draw a rough outline of the tree, with 'before wiring' and 'after wiring' versions. Don't worry about the quality of your sketch, as it's only for your reference.

Advance planning will dictate the direction and placement of the wire and will lessen the chance of the tree being damaged and the possibility of die-back. When a branch is bent, the cells on the outside of the curve are stretched long and thin while those on the inside of the curve become cramped. If the branch is repeatedly bent first one way and then the other, the effect may be to damage those cells beyond repair.

However, do not be afraid of wiring your tree just because you are a beginner and you consider that your wiring is not up to scratch. It may be controversial, but bad wiring is still better at getting character in your tree than no wiring at all.

Preparation

Before you start to wire to shape it is necessary to prepare the tree. First, the tree should be healthy and should not have been recently re-potted. Do not over-stress an already stressed tree. However, it is acceptable to wire a healthy tree and then re-pot it soon after wiring has been completed.

To prepare the tree for wiring, shorten any over-long branches and clear away any unwanted twigs, foliage or needles. This will make the structure of the tree clearer and make wiring easier. On pines, do not just pull off the unwanted needles – you may pull the undeveloped buds with them and these are all required for the back-budding and twigging that is necessary if a tree is to look mature. No budding is wanted underneath any of the branches so these needles can just be pulled away but in other areas you should cut the needles away carefully with a pair of scissors. Junipers also often have needles or scales growing along the branches. Clear these away so that the branch being wired is devoid of greenery.

Before wiring and re-potting, this Japanese White Pine was pretty but looked more like a hedgehog than a tree. Wiring and re-potting led to great improvements (TOP AND BOTTOM RIGHT)

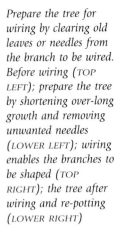

Prepare the tree for wiring by clearing old leaves or needles from the branch to be wired. Before wiring (TOP LEFT); prepare the tree by shortening over-long growth and removing unwanted needles (LOWER LEFT); wiring enables the branches to be shaped (TOP RIGHT); the tree after wiring and re-potting (LOWER RIGHT)

Equipment checklist: wiring bonsai trees		
Ideal	**Alternative**	**Purpose**
Copper wire of varying thickness and length	Aluminium wire of varying thickness and length	For shaping branches and trunks
Wire cutters		For cutting wire to length
Pliers		For finishing off ends of wire
Raffia		For wrapping around branches to prevent damage
Water spray	Recycled household spray	To mist-spray tree after wiring
Wound sealant	Petroleum jelly	To cover bark wounds

Using Wire

Purposes

Wire may be used for three purposes in bonsai design and care:

1. to shape the tree;
2. to wire it into its pot so that it is firmly held; and
3. to wire the pot on to a stand so that it does not fall off in bad weather.

Types of Wire

Garden wire is unsatisfactory for wiring bonsai trees as it looks unsightly and rusts easily, which renders it fairly useless. Green plastic-covered garden wire has some use as it can, in an emergency, be utilized for wiring trees into their pots

Half-kilogram coils of anodized aluminium wire of various diameters

when re-potting, but it should not be used for wiring branches.

Professionals use copper wire for wiring their bonsai trees into shape. However, it is expensive, can be difficult to apply and even more difficult to remove. Annealing is a process that alters the copper's crystal structure and softens it, making it easier to apply. Annealing involves heating the wire until it glows a cherry-red colour, and then allowing it to cool. Whether it is cooled quickly or slowly will not alter its degree of malleability, but plunging the hot wire into cold water will cause any outer debris to crack off, leaving the copper clean and bright. During the process of wrapping the wire around the branch, its crystal structure will change again and it will harden to such an extent that it can only be removed without damaging the tree by cutting it off carefully in small sections.

Copper wire should not be used on some varieties of tree, such as *prunus* and, although its properties may help to hinder the growth rate of a tree, care should be taken when using it for wiring trees into pots. If you think that contact with copper may damage your tree, either use an alternative type of wire or wrap the copper wire in florist's tape before using it.

Copper's main benefits are its strength – which means that thinner gauges can be used – and its appearance; it wears well and develops a pleasing green patina as it ages. However, wire is sold by weight, so copper's extra density means that there is less length of wire to the kilogram than with aluminium wire.

Anodized aluminium wire is attractive, user-friendly and therefore the most widely used in bonsai design. The thinner gauges are of a pleasing bronze colour, which harmonizes with the

Wire of various gauges and types have been used to wire this pine tree into shape

bark of most trees, and it is easy both to apply and to remove. Thicker gauges of anodized aluminium wire are available but they are not always easy to obtain. The more readily available types have a tendency to be bright silver, which can be somewhat obtrusive in the overall look of the tree.

Aluminium wire is only slightly cheaper to buy than copper wire but it proves much more economical. It is reusable, because it can be unwound from a tree rather than having to be cut off in small pieces. However, you should carefully inspect any salvaged aluminium wire before reusing it, as it has a tendency to break at any points where it has previously been bent or stressed. It is frustrating to have a length of wire break half-way along a branch.

Suppliers

Copper wire and anodized aluminium wire can be bought in short lengths from most garden centres or in kilogram or half-kilogram coils from specialist dealers. Unsurprisingly, it is much more economical to buy kilogram coils than the short pre-packaged lengths. There is an increasing number of suppliers of suitable wire, many of which offer mail order.

Thickness of Wire

Gauges (thickness) of wire generally progress in half-millimetre stages between 0.5mm and 6.0mm, which is a gauge strong enough to

was, it is too thin; if it is much harder to bend, it is too thick and may be difficult to apply.

Sometimes it is better to use two lengths of a thinner-gauge wire than to use one thick one. If you apply the wire and it does not hold the branch as you wish it to be held, do not remove the first piece. Instead, apply a second length of wire immediately parallel to it and touching it. Generally, copper wire will be between one-sixth and one-third of the thickness of the branch. Aluminium wire has less strength, and will be from one-third to one-half as thick.

If one length of wire does not hold the branch, add another length of wire parallel to the first. A small pad has been used to protect the branch at a point where the wire might rub

Length of Wire to Use

When wiring a trunk, the length of wire needed is approximately twice the length of the trunk. When wiring a branch you will need a length of wire up to approximately one and a half times the length of the branch. Allow extra wire for anchorage.

If two branches are to be wired, allow enough wire for each branch plus the length needed to wrap around the trunk to cover the distance between the two branches.

The gauge of wire used to shape this tree gets progressively smaller as the branches become thinner

handle the most reluctant of branches or trunks. If a wire stronger than 6mm is needed, it may be better to use several lengths of a thinner gauge or use an alternative method, change your design or select another tree to fit it.

The gauge of wire needed for wiring is largely determined by the type of wire, and how radically you want to bend the branch, plus its age and its resistance to change. For normal usage, the wire needed should have a little more resistance to bending than the branch you are working on. First, bend the branch lightly to feel how much pressure you have to apply to get it to bend a little. Now feel your wire and bend it slightly. If it is easier to bend than the branch

When to Apply Wire

Although the main wiring of your tree will be done in the earlier stages of its training, it is probable that some branch or twig of it will have to be wired as part of its general maintenance even when it is mature. It is advisable to stop watering your tree for a couple of days before you want to wire it. The loss of moisture will make it more flexible, but you should only do this if you are confident that the tree will not suffer from drought, and will recover easily. Do not wire your tree just after you have

Rule of thumb guide: wiring trees		
Type of Tree	**When to Wire**	**How Long to Retain Wire**
Conifer	In winter	Eight to ten months upwards
Deciduous	Between spring and autumn	Four to six months
Flowering tree	Between spring and autumn	Three to four months
Fruit tree	Between spring and autumn	Three to four months
Indoor bonsai	When necessary	One month
Mame tree (all varieties)	Before re-potting	Four to six months

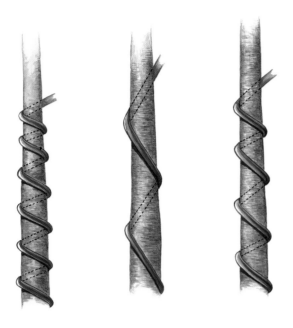

re-potted it; give it time to recover so that you do not over-stress it.

Your tree may be wired at any time of the year, but there are times when wiring will be less harmful. The best time for wiring conifers is between late autumn and early spring, making it an ideal task for those long winter evenings. During these months the tree is dormant and, as it is still too early for the new buds to have swollen, little damage is likely to occur during the process.

Pruning methods are usually used to shape deciduous trees, but it is sometimes necessary to wire small areas or wayward branches into shape. During the cold winter months deciduous trees can become very brittle and the risk of branches breaking during the process is greatly increased. Any wiring on deciduous trees is best done in late autumn before the tree becomes dormant, or left until the spring when it is active but before its buds have broken open and its leaves are beginning to show. However, if you have been adventurous and defoliated your tree in midsummer (*see* Chapter 7), it can be wired immediately after the leaves have been cut off. The tree's growth will have been checked and its energy devoted to producing a new set of leaves.

Indoor bonsai are much less resilient than outdoor trees and, as they have never been subjected to harsh weather conditions, their bark is much more tender and more easily damaged by wiring. It may, therefore, be advisable to protect the bark of an indoor tree by wrapping it in raffia before wire is applied. Check the wiring every week and remove it immediately should any damage to the bark become evident.

How to Apply Wire

The wire must be firmly anchored to stop it slipping and the tree should always be wired from the bottom up, starting with the trunk. After the trunk has been wired, the branches and twigs can be tackled, with the lower branches being wired first and the crown last. This will allow the branches to be properly placed and the new shape to emerge as you progress upwards through the tree.

Wire is applied spirally in either a clockwise or anti-clockwise direction, depending on which way you want to move the branches. It must be wound at an angle of 45 degrees. If the angle is wider than 45 degrees there will be an insufficient number of turns and not enough strength in the wiring to hold the branch. If the angle is sharper than 45 degrees, the coils will be too close together and there is a danger that it might have cut off essential flows and nutrients. Twigs and branches grow where they wish to, therefore the 45-degree angle rule cannot be rigidly applied and judgement is needed to ensure that no growing parts are trapped under the wire.

Apply the wire with a constant tension – not too tight and not too loose. The wire should hold the branch firmly but still leave room for growth. If you are right-handed, hold the wire in your right hand and firmly hold the pot, tree or branch to stabilize it with your left; vice versa for left-handed people.

When you have wired the branch to the end, cut off any excess wire that may be protruding beyond the end of the branch as it can be both unsightly and dangerous. Alternatively, use the pliers to bend the wire back under the branch for a short distance to form a small loop. The wire under the branch will be unobtrusive and can provide a small 'handle' to get hold of when you want to remove the wire at a later date.

Wiring Techniques

Wiring a Trunk

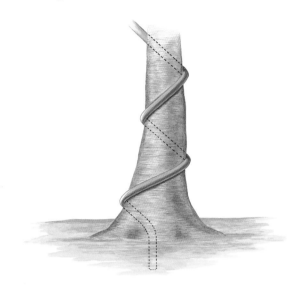

Before starting to wind wire around the trunk, it is necessary to anchor the wire. If the wire is not firmly fixed it will move about as you wind it around the trunk and damage the bark. To anchor the wire, simply push one end of it as far into the soil as it will go, as close to the trunk as possible, taking care not to damage the tree's roots. If the tree is in a deep pot, pushing the wire about 2in (5cm) into the soil should be sufficient to hold it in place. The tree's root structure may restrict the number of places where this can be done, but it is preferable for visual reasons to push the wire into the soil at the back of the tree, so that it is less obtrusive.

Having anchored the wire, carefully wind it around the trunk at a consistent angle of 45 degrees, making sure that the wire is neither too tight nor too loose, and that no branches are trapped or constricted. When bending the trunk to shape, work slowly and methodically. If you get it right first time, you are less likely to cause damage to the tree by repeatedly changing the direction of the bend. Look at your sketch and try to follow it.

Radical changes may call for strong arms and stronger wire. If you are intending to make a sharp bend, remember to protect the trunk by wrapping it with raffia or a similar material before you start wiring.

Cracks may appear in the bark on the outside

of a new bend. Cover the cracks with cut paste or petroleum jelly to seal them and minimize the possibility of fungal attacks.

Wiring a Branch

Older branches of trees will have been brought downwards by their own weight, lack of light will have stripped their inner leaves, and wind and weather will have had their effect over countless winters. To simulate this and bring character to the branch, you will need to bend the branch up and down and also bend it from side to side.

Again, anchor wires so that they are firmly held. This is easiest to achieve if you are wiring two branches with a single length of wire – one branch will act as a lever against the other branch (*see* diagram overleaf). If only one branch is to be wired, wrap the wire around the trunk a couple of times, following the line of any existing wiring and taking care that no wires cross.

Always make sure that there is protecting wire on the outside of every bend. For example, if the branch is being bent upwards, wire should be under the branch directly beneath the bend. If it being bent downwards, the wire should be directly above the bend, on the top of the branch. If bending to one side or another, the wire must always be on the outside of the bend (*see* diagram overleaf). Without the protecting wire, it is likely that the branch will crack or break when you bend it and all your efforts may be lost.

LEFT: *Firmly anchor the wire in the pot, preferably at the back of the tree*

RIGHT: *If radical changes are to be made, wrap the trunk in raffia before wiring and bending it: it took two men with strong arms to bend this trunk, but with good preparation the bend was achieved without cracking*

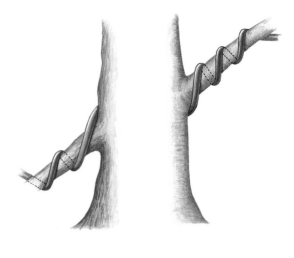

Another point to take into consideration is that there should be no side-branches on the inside of any bends that you create.

As with trunks, when attempting to bend very thick branches it may be wise first to wrap the branch in raffia in order to lessen the chance of the branch cracking or breaking. Thicker branches have a tendency to be more brittle than their younger relatives and require much more pressure to be applied to alter their shape. This makes them more prone to snapping and makes precautionary measures more than worth the time and effort. Experienced bonsai designers may use branch splitters to make the job of bending easier but these should only be used if you are confident of your skills. Remember, once you split a branch it usually stays split.

Bark may also crack on the outside of any bends and should be treated with cut paste or petroleum jelly in order to seal the wounds.

Lowering a Branch

There is more than one way of using wire to lower a branch. The wire can be fixed to a stone, which is then attached to the branch; bearing the weight of the stone continuously for several months may permanently alter the branch's angle. Another way is to wire the branch to a fixed point such as the trunk or the pot and then to shorten the wire as required by twisting it with the tommy-bar until the desired angle is achieved. In this way the branch can be lowered progressively. Do not fix the wire too tightly to the branch and protect the branch from damage with a small pad or piece of tubing.

Removing Wire

When to Remove Wire

Ideally, wire should be left on the tree until the branch has set in the shape you were seeking, but the time will vary according to the age and variety of the tree. As older wood is more resistant to change and needs longer to adopt a new shape than younger wood, a trunk will take longer to follow a new direction than branches and twigs. Generally, a trunk will take shape within a year, branches in about four months and twigs in about two or three months.

Even this mame Japanese Black Pine has had its branches wrapped in raffia before bending took place

LOWER LEFT: Hardened wire should be cut away from the branch in small pieces

As a rule of thumb, wire can be left on conifers for eight to ten months but should only be left on deciduous trees for up to four months. If the tree is mature and very slow-growing, wire can be left on almost indefinitely, but it is best to remove wire after eighteen months, and rewire again at a later date. In this case try to give your tree a wire-free holiday, a time to flex and stretch, before you wire it again.

Deciduous trees grow rapidly in the summer months and any wiring will need to be checked regularly to ensure that it is not biting into the bark. Deciduous trees such as beech or *Zelkova* heal less easily from wire damage than coniferous trees, and scars on deciduous tree are much more likely to be permanent.

Conifers, because of (or in spite of) their flexibility are notoriously difficult to coax into retaining a new shape and often revert to their old shape once wire has been removed. If this happens, it will be necessary to rewire the section. When you start to rewire the tree, wind the wire in the opposite direction from your last efforts in order to minimize any damage.

In a truly neglected tree, wire can become invisible as bark grows over it and it becomes absorbed by the tree. If the wire is so completely embedded that it cannot be removed without

Branches can be lowered by using wire attached to a fixed point. A branch of the omono Dawn Redwood (TOP) has been lowered by fixing it to the trunk with wire. Several branches of the chumono pine (BELOW) have been attached to a ring of wire running around the pot

causing fatal damage, leaving it on the branch may be the lesser of two evils. Eventually the affected area can be gradually pruned away. Wire left on too long can cause unsightly lumps on the branch, with localized swelling at points where natural flows have been interrupted.

This chumono-sized twin-trunk juniper has been carefully wired into the traditional asymmetrical triangular shape

This chumono larch has a very different shape from the juniper but also fits into the asymmetrical triangle

However, as wire is applied in a spiral rather than a ring, nutrients should still be able to flow through the branch.

Anodized aluminium wire can usually be successfully removed by simple unwinding. Copper wire will have set hard and you will have to exert too much pressure on the tree to remove it in the same way. Instead, cut it off in small pieces using sharp wire cutters, taking care to snip only through the wire and not the tree.

Aftercare

Before the tree was wired it should have been healthy and well fed; remember, sick or newly re-potted trees should not be wired. Immediately after wiring, the tree will be partially in shock and will require love and attention.

Water it well, especially if water was restricted before wiring. Cosset it by placing it in a cold frame for frost protection for winter wiring, or in a shaded place away from the sun after summer wiring. In summer, if the tree is in leaf, mist-spray it regularly to reduce any stress that may have been placed on its root system. In winter, remember that it will not recover from its stress until the spring comes.

13 Rocks and Landscapes

General Principles

Rocks come in all shapes and sizes and care should be taken over their selection. Whether the rock is for a root-over-rock planting, a root-on-rock planting, or simply to be used as part of a landscape, choosing the 'right' rock is as important as choosing the right pot. If the selection isn't made carefully enough, the 'root-over-rock' may irreverently be termed as 'root-over-brick' or 'root-over-pebble'.

Find a rock that has many fissures, an interesting shape, sits solidly when in position and is of the size you want for the finished tree. This may sound obvious, but it is a point often overlooked. The tree will grow but the rock will not, and sometimes years of work can be lost when a tree completely engulfs its host.

Rocks should be interesting and attractive in their own right, even on their own, with nothing planted on or over them. Glittery rocks and marbles are said to be unsuitable for bonsai, as they detract from the trees. However, a larch on a piece of white quartzite has been seen to be most impressive.

Once the rock has been chosen, take time to select its most interesting aspect. Much will depend on whether the rock is intended for a root-over-rock or a root-on-rock planting, but the most pleasing viewing angle is usually the one that has the most dramatic line. If the rock does not sit naturally and firmly at the desired angle, level it by making a foot with a resinous type of car-filler or something similar. It will eventually be out of sight at the back of the rock or below compost or water level. If genuine rocks are used, rock plantings can be exceedingly heavy and difficult to manhandle and assistance might be needed in moving them about.

Choose your rocks carefully: this lovely trident maple has formed a clump and completely engulfed the rock over which it was growing

As well as personal preference, practicalities relating to availability have to be taken into account when choosing a rock. The rock planting on page 47 utilizes a beautiful red granite imported from Zimbabwe, but it is unlikely that you will find this type of rock in your local garden centre. The same applies to the Japanese imported Ibigawa volcanic rock used for the root-over-rock planting on page 47. However, both types of rock may be available from specialist bonsai centres.

Ibigawa is ideal for all types of rock planting as it has interesting contours, nooks and crannies, and has colour variation. The rock is treated with an acid solution, which eats away the softer parts leaving fantastic contours. Often the best surface will already have been selected and the rock may have been given a pre-sawn

Imported Ibigawa compound volcanic rock

Resin-based imitation rock

Alternatives to expensive imported rocks can be found in local garden centres: (LEFT TO RIGHT) weathered limestone; sandstone; tufa

Root-on-Rock

The process of creating a root-on-rock planting is, with few exceptions, the same, regardless of the type of rock used. The three inexpensive rocks pictured below were found in piles of rockery stone at a garden centre. If you have a strong back and live near a rocky area, it would add interest to your planting if you were to collect rock yourself.

The first of the pictured rocks is a weather-worn piece of limestone, the second is sand-stone and the third is formed from tufa. Limestone is alkaline and therefore not suitable for acid-loving plants, but eminently suitable for lime-loving yews. Sandstone is neutral and suitable for any species of tree. As they are soft, sedimentary types of rock, sandstone and limestone are likely to weather and erode and consequently are not entirely suitable for long-term use. However, they offer an excellent and inexpensive starting point from which to develop skills. ('Long-term' is, of course, a relative concept as the plantings are still likely to outlive the person who creates them.) Tufa is very soft, porous limestone, slowly formed from constantly dripping calcium carbonate-rich water. It is so soft that planting pockets are easily carved into it, but the softness also means that, unless great care is taken to protect it from knocks, lumps are easily broken off the finished planting.

For ease, the tree could be planted in a small crevice, but with firmly fixed retaining wires it can also be attached to an almost vertical sheer surface. On a tall rock, a tree is most likely to have a cascading or semi-cascading effect as it tumbles its way down the rock-face. The style lends itself to multiple plantings of the same species or of different species of

flat base. Other, more ordinary rocks, although perhaps less interesting in shape, are still emi-nently useful and are available locally from larger well-stocked garden centres.

Imitation rocks made of resin may not have as much character as originals, but they are useful inexpensive and lighter alternatives to the real thing. Cement-based 'rock' slabs (*see* pages 50 and 116) are easily made at home; for full instructions on their construction, *see* Chapter 15.

A different process is involved in root-over-rock and root-on-rock plantings. With root-over-rock, the roots flow over the rock and into the compost; with a root-on-rock, both the tree and compost remain entirely on the rock and never flow below it.

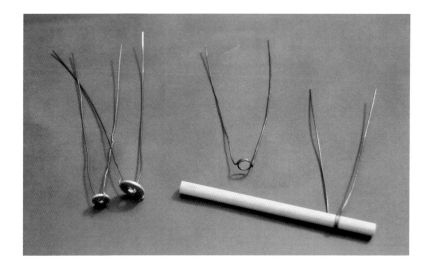

tree. Remember, whether the rock planting is for a single tree, or for a group of trees, it should always tell a story and evoke emotion.

When the rock and trees have been chosen, a method has to be found of anchoring the trees firmly into position on the rock. If a soft, porous rock such as tufa is being used this is not a problem, as free-draining planting pockets are easily carved into it. If the rock is hard, this is not an option, unless electrical equipment and specialized drill bits are used. With hard rock, the most suitable method of anchoring trees is to thread wire through metal washers, or to twist wires so that they have a flat base, and then glue them into place on the rock. Various strong fast-hardening epoxy-resins, available from DIY stores, will give a good bond between the wire and the rock. Before glueing the wires in place, clean the rock thoroughly, with a pressure hose if necessary, to ensure that there is no loose debris.

The open, free-draining composts generally used for re-potting bonsai trees are not suitable for rock-planted trees as they do not stay in position on surfaces that are more often vertical than horizontal. This is where all the siftings left over from the general compost can be used; sedge peat is better than moss peat as it is of a stickier consistency. Take the peat and clay siftings and mix them with water until a putty-like 'peat muck' is formed. This will give a suitable planting medium that will hold together and, if covered with moss after the tree

has been planted, will stay in place during watering.

Large rocks can be extremely weighty and difficult to handle, so put them in place before they are planted up and plant *in situ*. Smaller rocks can be planted up beforehand and then moved into place. Select the rock's best angle and make sure that it sits firmly. Study the composition of the rock and select plants and trees that will thrive on it, rather than struggle for existence. For further information root-on-rock plantings *see* Chapter 15.

Tufa is soft, and planting pockets can easily be carved out with a coal chisel

Make fixing points for retaining wires by threading wire through metal washers or twisting wires so that they have a flat base that can be glued to the rock

The tufa upended and planted with a mame-sized Zelkova

Equipment checklist: root-on-rock plantings	
Item	**Purpose**
Suitable rock	Of good shape and size
Suitable tree/s	For rock planting
Peat muck	In which to plant the tree
Wire	For fixing the tree to the rock and stapling moss to the compost
Pliers	To bend and tighten the wire
Moss	To cover the peat muck and enhance the planting

Root-over-Rock

To train a root-over-rock tree, it is better to start when the tree is young and pliable. Ideally, use a tree whose roots have been allowed to extend so that they can be easily wrapped around the chosen rock. Eventually, the root will flow over the rock and form feeding roots below the rock.

There are various ways in which the root-over-rock effect can be achieved. A large tree can be fixed over the rock and bound into place with raffia or wire. Compost is then heaped over the exposed roots, and covered in moss. The

Procedure for root-on-rock planting

1. Select a suitable rock and find its best angle, then glue tree-retaining wires in place. (This is the piece of limestone shown on page 128.)

3. Cover all roots with peat muck, add moss and staple it into place (*see* Chapter 15).

2. Cover planting areas with peat muck, then start to fix material in place.

4. Mist-spray foliage and water well.

Equipment checklist: root-over-rock plantings

Item	Purpose
Tree	To plant over the rock
Suitable-sized rock	Over which to place the roots
Grafting tape or polythene strip cut from a carrier bag	To bind the roots and stop them spreading out
Compost mix of peat and grit	In which to bury the rock
Deep flowerpot	Deep enough to take the rock and still have room for the development of roots

Procedure for creating a root-over-rock tree

1. Select a rock of a suitable size for the finished tree.

2. Spread the roots of the seedling tree evenly over the chosen rock in a pleasing manner.

3. Completely wrap both roots and rock in polythene strip.

4. Plant both rock and roots in the ground or in a deep flowerpot.

5. Leave the ensemble for as long as it takes for the roots to firmly grip the rock. This can take a couple of years.

6. When sufficient lower roots have formed, the ensemble can be planted up in a bonsai pot.

ABOVE: This may be lovely but it is a miniature garden not a miniature landscape, and not what you are trying to achieve

RIGHT: Get ideas for landscapes from holiday photos: this is Avebury Circle, Wiltshire, on a bleak December morning. The small figure at the side highlights the size of the massive rocks that form this ancient monument

roots will eventually grip the rock but this is a slow process.

Alternatively, for a faster result, the tree can be fixed over the rock and have its roots confined so that outward growth is prohibited, forcing the roots to grip the rock as they thicken. Grafting tape is ideal for binding purposes but is not easy to find in non-specialist outlets. An alternative strip can be cut from a carrier bag.

When choosing a rock and a tree, consider what you want as an end result. The process is slow and prior consideration will eliminate later disappointment. Choose a rock with many fissures to which roots can cling and a tree that will lend itself to this style.

Landscapes

General Principles

With a bit of planning, a few rocks, bits of wood, a variety of seedling trees and a few spare hours a magnificent landscape can be created in a small tray. Landscapes and group plantings are both comprised of numerous small trees, and the main difference between them is that group plantings, regardless of the number and type of trees used, always resemble parts of forests; on the other hand, the range of possibilities for landscapes is almost limitless. In landscapes, the intention is not to create a miniature garden but to represent miles

of sweeping vista in a very small space. A landscape is also one of the rare cases when different types of tree can be combined to dramatic effect.

Ideas for Landscapes

If you intend to use materials you already have, your choice of landscape may be restricted. If you are starting from scratch, anything is possible. Consider creating a representation of mountains and valleys, rolling hills with distant trees, copses and hedgerows, lakeside woodlands, windswept cliffs, indoor tropical rainforests or deserts, a memorable view seen while on holiday or one that has a significant meaning to you.

To get ideas, look at your holiday photographs or pictures in travel books and magazines. Draw a sketch of what pleases you. Do not slavishly produce an exact copy of what you see; the aim is to use perspective to give an impression of the chosen scenery in a small space. Unless you have a competition in mind, the landscape has only to please you and nobody else.

Trays and Containers

Landscapes can be created in any type of container that is made of a plant-friendly material, situated in a position where it will receive light and moisture. It is an excellent way for the flat dweller with a window box or balcony to enjoy a variety of living postcards. Before choosing a container consider the type of landscape that is to be represented. Specialist bonsai trays, artificial slabs, seed trays, drilled drainage saucers, window boxes and tree stumps may all be used. Sinks and planting troughs are too deep, and should be kept for alpine and miniature gardens rather than bonsai landscapes. Gravel trays of various sizes and colours can be bought cheaply from all garden centres and DIY stores. However, if the tray is both large and plastic, it will be brittle and might require a support frame to prevent it cracking when it is moved.

To avoid waterlogging and root rot, sufficiently large drainage holes must be provided if something other than the customary bonsai tray is to be used to house the bonsai landscape. At the same time drill small holes to accommodate any retaining wires that may be needed. Thread wire through the small holes and cover the drainage holes with screening mesh to prevent loss of precious compost and to deny pests easy access to the tray.

Landscape Materials

Creating a landscape presents an opportunity to use unwanted trees that have self-seeded in your flowerbeds or have sprouted from unrecovered squirrel hiding places. Don't forget those inevitable bonsai failures from early attempts at styling that have been relegated to the bottom of the garden. While none of these trees might be good enough to stand as bonsai trees on their own, or be of the right shape to be incorporated into group plantings, they could be combined with other trees in a landscape. (If you do find a tree that has a potentially good trunk line or root flare, save it and develop it as a specimen tree.)

Due to the time involved in putting a large-scale design together, the roots of trees will be exceptionally vulnerable to drying out. To avoid problems, prepare the tray and complete all 'hard' landscaping before taking the trees from their pots.

Positioning Rocks

When the tray has been prepared, any rocks that are to be incorporated into the design should be put in place. Over the lifespan of the landscape, changes will occur in the variety and positioning of the trees – some trees will die and some grow too big for the design – but, unless the whole landscape is being redesigned, it is unlikely that the positioning of the rocks will be altered.

Choose rocks of a similar colour and stabilize them by sinking the bases as low as possible. This will not only stop the rocks moving about but will lead to greater realism; they will look as though they are coming out of the ground rather than sitting on top of it. Place the largest rocks at the front of the composition with the smaller rocks at the rear, to give the impression that the rocks are receding into the distance. For the most natural look, arrange the rocks so that any fault lines in the rocks run in the same direction, complementing rather than confusing the design.

A representation of Avebury Circle newly created on an artificial slab: an illusion of distance is achieved by placing a small rock slightly behind the large rocks giving the impression that it was of the same size but much further away. Sandstone, Zelkova, ferns, moss and a few alpine plants have all been used

Compost

The compost mixture required for the planting will depend on the variety of trees that are being used. (*See* Chapter 8 for details of compost mixes for various trees.) In large landscapes this is less of a problem than in smaller ones. If the planting is large enough the compost mix can be varied to suit the trees in various parts of the tray. Adding grit to one area will make it more free-draining and adding more peat to another area will make it more water-retentive. However, if the tray is small, it may be wiser only to use trees that require similar growing conditions.

Planting Trees and 'Shrubs'

When the 'hard' landscaping has been completed, attention can be given to the trees and plants. Dealing with one tree at a time, but keeping the whole design in mind, trim the tops of the trees to shape, shortening branches that are over-long. Do not remove too many branches until you are sure that they are not wanted. Unwanted branches can be cut off later when the tree is in place but cannot be reattached once amputated.

When the trees have been shaped to your satisfaction, remove them from their pots and, one at a time, carefully trim and spread their roots so that they will fit neatly into the tray. This is easier if the trees have already had some bonsai training and have developed flat root systems. However, as seedling trees seldom have a dense root system, they are normally usable once the taproots have been removed. Spray the trees regularly to keep them moist and protect any roots that are likely to be exposed to the air for a long time by popping them into plastic bags.

Consult the original sketch of the landscape and loosely place the trees in position. This is where changes are likely to occur between your first plan and what will actually work with the material you have. Don't worry about fine-tuning the design at this stage, just move the trees about until the balance you want has been achieved, then start to plant. Stand back, study the composition from various angles and ask questions of it. Is it convincing? Is anything missing? Does it need extra rocks, more trees or different trees? Do the trees complement or conflict with each other?

Starting with the dominant trees, wire them into place and cover their roots with suitable compost. Then, working in one area at time, arrange the smaller trees around them, wiring them in and adding compost as required until all the trees are in place. If everything is as it should be, then you can start adding the underplanting of mosses and ferns. Brush off any excess material, put any coloured gravel that might be needed in place and water the landscape thoroughly.

Your landscape will need to be protected from harsh sunlight for a few weeks and will require maintenance in the future but, on the balcony or in the garden, it will give years of pleasure.

For an example of how to create a landscape in a plastic greenhouse gravel tray, *see* Chapter 15.

14 Groups and Rafts

If they are to be used for a group planting, take cuttings from only one tree to ensure that all the new trees have the same characteristics

General Principles

Group plantings resemble part of a forest – a place where, if you were the right tiny size, you could wander, stop for a picnic and marvel at the power or grace of the trees. Reflect upon the way in which the trees in a group search for light, and how this affects their shape (*see* Chapter 2). When putting groups together, this factor must be taken into account. You should also adhere to the asymmetrical triangle if the planting is to look realistic.

A group should be of an unequal number of trees, with trunks of varying thickness and lengths. They should be unevenly spaced, so that they look as though that is how nature, rather than the Forestry Commission, intended them to look. Ranks of trees never look convincing. Ideally, the trees would be of a wide age range with many already having undergone bonsai training, but this is not always feasible. The stock in garden centres has usually come from the same source, so that all the trees are the same age and of the same height. Beginners are unlikely to have a ready stock of aged bonsai trees to hand. In this case, they may make several different plantings of the same species of tree, with the aim of eventually putting them together as a larger and more varied group.

Let the group tell a story and the illusion will be complete. Is the forest to be dark and dense, somewhere trolls reside, or a place of light and air where fairies live? Coniferous plantings tend to be the former whereas deciduous plantings tend to be the latter. The colour of the foliage also affects the mood of the planting; light green leaves say one thing, while dark green needles or scales say something quite different.

Omono-sized group of Japanese maples

Unless all the trees from which the group is comprised were grown from cuttings or air layers taken from the same parent tree, there will be variations in growing habit, colour, leaf or flower forms. Another way of creating a group of trees, with identical characteristics throughout the planting, is to create a raft. In a raft, a tree is laid flat and its branches become the trunks of new trees. Initially they are all fed from the same root, but new roots eventually form along the length of the old trunk, using the same principle as for air layering (*see* page 138).

Groups

Unless your group is to be particularly large, start it off in a training pot or seed tray. Mature groups should be in shallow pots or on slabs; putting the group in a deeper pot to start off with will allow the roots of the trees to recover before being placed permanently in a shallow pot. It will also give you time to see how the group develops so that the right pot can be chosen.

Basically, the rules for group plantings are as follows:

* trees should be of the same species;
* an uneven number of trees should be used;
* trees should have trunks of varying thickness and height;
* trees should be unevenly spaced;
* a dominant tree should be in the foreground and set slightly higher than the other trees;

Forest planting of Zelkova on an artificial slab

This group of pines has been planted in a seed tray and wired into shape. It will stay like this until the branches have thickened and the foliage pads have developed before being transferred to a permanent pot

Equipment checklist: group plantings	
Item	**Purpose**
Uneven number of trees of the same species	From which to make the planting
Pruning scissors	To remove unwanted branches and foliage
Wire	To wire the trunks and branches to shape and fix the trees into the seed tray
Wire-cutters	For cutting the wire
Seed tray	In which to plant the group
Compost	In which to plant the trees

Procedure for group plantings

1. Gather together an uneven number of trees of the same species and prepare a seed tray for planting.

2. Take them from their pots, trim off excess roots and cut off any foliage that is growing directly upwards or downwards. Do not remove any major branches, as they may be needed.

3. If coniferous trees are being used, wire all the trunks and major branches.

4. Study the trunks and try the trees in various positions before deciding on the shape of the group.

5. Once the positioning decision has been made, trim back the roots, fix the trees firmly in the seed tray at the correct angles, remove any unwanted branches and bend the remaining branches to shape.

Omono-sized forest planting in a Japanese bonsai centre

- the inner part of the planting should be treated as though it were a single tree, with little foliage and no branches crossing or interfering with other trees;
- trunks should not obscure each other; and
- the outer part of the planting should fit within an asymmetrical triangular shape.

Deciduous trees can usually be pruned into a desired shape, but to attain a desired shape with coniferous trees it will be necessary to wire all of the trees before putting the group together. The trees then can be bent to shape when the overall position of each tree is known. Not all trees in groups survive the initial styling and there may be casualties, therefore it is advisable to have a few extra trees of the same species available should they be needed.

Rafts

A bushy tree is better than a sparse one for starting a raft planting as it will give a better choice of material from which to form the trunks of new trees. It could take a long time for roots to form from the trunk so make the planting in a seed tray or training pot. The old root of the tree has to be retained until the new roots grow and this can be unsightly.

Raft-style Japanese maple

Equipment checklist: creating a raft	
Item	**Purpose**
Suitable tree	Raw material for raft
Knob-cutters or secateurs	To cut off unwanted branches
Wire	To wire branches upright and wire tree into place
Wire-cutters	For cutting wire
Seed tray	In which to plant the raft
Grit/peat compost	In which to plant the raft

Procedure for creating a raft

1. Select a healthy tree that has a sufficient number of branches to provide several trunks.

2. Remove the tree from its pot and cut away all thick and all long, straggly roots.

3. Clear out the deadwood around the trunk so that all possibilities can be assessed. Select the side that

is to be developed and that which is to be cleared of growth. One side of the tree often has fewer branches than the other.

4. Cut away all branches on one side of the tree. A knob-cutter helps to give a clean, concave cut to the trunk.

5. Place a polythene bag around the roots of the tree to stop them drying out and wire all the remaining branches into an upright position.

6. Cover the bottom of a seed tray with a drainage layer of gravel and thread retaining wires through the drainage holes so that the tree can be firmly held in place. Measure the tree against the seed tray to make sure that it will fit, including the remainder of the root.

Procedure for creating a raft *continued*

7. To encourage new roots to form from the old trunk, cover the wounds to the trunk with hormone rooting compound. If only a few branches were removed, make further cuts into the trunk, ensuring that they penetrate the cambium, and treat them with hormone rooting compound in the same way.

8. Put a layer of compost on top of the drainage grit, remove the polythene bag from the roots and lay the tree on the bed of compost with the branches facing upwards. Wire it into place and add the rest of the compost mixture, making sure that the old root is completely covered.

9. Water thoroughly and place in a shaded area.

10. Do not waste the branches that were cut off; pot them up as cuttings for another group planting.

11. Rooting is indicated when the new 'trees' are showing signs of growth. Only when you are sure that new roots have formed should the old root be cut off.

12. The procedure for preparing a sinuous style planting is the same but, instead of the trunk being laid out flat and straight, it should be pinned down, as its name suggests, in a more wavy line.

15 Projects

Project 1

Aim: to create a bonsai from a garden-centre pine tree

Materials:
Bushy pine tree with an interesting trunk (Mountain Pine)
Turntable
Pruning scissors
Knob-cutters (or secateurs)
Wire-cutters
Wire
Wound-sealing compound
Bonsai pot or training pot (over-sized)
Compost
Wedge
Moss for finishing

Mountain Pine

Method:
1. Rotate the tree until the best 'front' is found.
2. Garden-centre trees have usually been planted fairly deeply and there is often quite a bit of trunk below compost level. This needs to be viewed to get a more complete picture of how the tree should develop. If you intend to re-pot the tree as soon as it is styled, take it from its pot and assess its root system. Cut back the roots

and put a polythene bag over them to prevent them from drying out. If the tree is to remain in its pot, then, if possible, cut the top off the pot and scrape away the compost until the bottom of the trunk is revealed.
3. Study the trunk line of the tree before cutting off any branches and finalize ideas on its proposed style. Branches can be

TOP LEFT AND LOWER LEFT: *The tree's trunk line should be studied before making any decisions about its proposed style*

TOP RIGHT: *Cut off shoots and branches that are growing straight up or straight down*

MIDDLE RIGHT: *Cut long shoots back to a new growing point*

Use cloth or paper to decide which branches to remove

altered, thickened and shaped but the trunk is more difficult to alter.

4. Cut off everything that is growing straight up or straight down. Shorten over-long shoots. Cut back to a new shoot if possible so that it can take over as a growing point.

5. Thin out the needles on the branches. Twigs may have needles, but branches should not; needles on a branch will make it look immature.

6. Select the branches to be kept. If there is indecision over the removal of a branch, cover it with a cloth or piece of paper in order to assess the effect of its removal. Remove unwanted branches with a knob-cutter or secateurs. Remember that if the tree is not to be 'flat', allowance must be made for back branches to give it depth. The further up the trunk, the thinner and shorter the branch should be. The branch-pruning will encourage back-budding to

take place, which will later add density to the foliage pads.

7. Cover all large cuts with wound-sealing compound.

8. Wire the whole tree, including branches and twigs.

9. Start to shape the lower branch first. Turn all foliage upwards, towards the light.

10. Move progressively up the tree placing all branches in relation to each other. This is

bonsai and not topiary so place pads of foliage at differing levels. A wedge placed under the roots will hold the tree at the angle of your choice.

11. Cut off all protruding bits of wire.

12. Prepare the pot. Until the tree has developed more it should be in an over-sized pot or a training pot.
13. Adding a bit of fresh sphagnum moss to the compost will help the roots to recover.
14. Pot up the tree and water it until the water can be seen coming through the drainage holes. Do not water it again until the compost has started to dry out.
15. Refine and reposition any branches that may have been misplaced during potting.
16. Place the tree in a protected position away from frost or strong sunlight.
17. As it is newly styled, the tree will have a 'twiggy' look. Over the next few years, work will need to be done on the foliage to encourage it to form pads.
18. Do not feed the tree until the roots have had time to recover, then feed regularly with an organic fertilizer.

LEFT: Wire all branches and twigs (TOP), turning the foliage upwards towards the light

MIDDLE: The prepared pot, with retaining wires

RIGHT: Sphagnum moss added to the compost will help the roots to recover

LEFT: Use a wedge to hold the tree at a particular angle

RIGHT: For the future, the tree needs its foliage pads developing and some more of the long growth shortening

Project 2

Aim: to create a root-on-rock style planting from garden-centre stone

Materials:
Postcard or photograph for inspiration
Rockery stone from a garden centre
Range of small trees
Resinous car-filler (for levelling, if required)
Epoxy resin
Wire

Wire-cutters
Pliers
Peat muck (made from peat and clay siftings)
Chopstick or knitting needle
Moss
Water tray (optional)

Method:

1. Wash the stone thoroughly, using a pressure hose if necessary.

2. View the stone from various angles until the most pleasing is found, and try it in its tray.

3. If the stone does not naturally stand straight at the required angle, stabilize it by making a foot at the rear of the stone with a resinous car-filler. Disguise the filler with sand or some other material that matches the chosen stone.

4. Glue retaining wires in place with epoxy resin. Put at least two wires in place for each planting area.

5. When the resin is dry, push peat muck into the planting area, firming it with a chopstick.
6. Suitably prune and shape the trees and wire them into place.
7. Tighten the wires with pliers.
8. Cover the roots of the trees with peat muck and firm it down.
9. Cover the peat muck with moss and staple it into place.
10. Water the planting thoroughly using a mist-sprayer. Rock plantings do not retain moisture well and should be watered more regularly than conventionally planted trees.
11. Place the rock in its tray. Adding water to the tray will increase the humidity around the trees.

Wiring the trees into place

The planted trees, their roots covered with peat muck

Project 3

Aim: to create a landscape in a gravel tray

Materials:
Photograph or postcard for inspiration
Gravel tray of chosen size
(If the gravel tray is large, 3 tree stakes for a support frame)
Rocks
Trees, shrubs, moss and ferns
Wire
Wire-cutters
Compost
Coloured aquarium gravel, if required, for water effect

Moss being wired into place

BOTTOM LEFT: *The finished planting, standing in its water-filled tray*

BELOW: *Inspiration for a landscape*

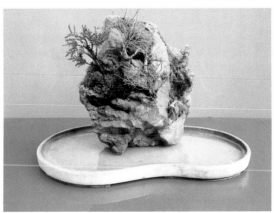

A brittle plastic tray and its essential wooden support

Method:

1. Prepare the tray by making drainage holes of a suitable size, and holes for retaining wires. Cover the holes and put the wire in place.
2. Unless measures are taken to provide support, a large plastic tray will crack under the weight of the planting materials when it is moved. Three wooden tree stakes, pre-treated with wood preservative, can provide the support needed to protect a 3-ft (90-cm) long tray. Cut off the pointed ends of all the stakes. Place two of the stakes side by side at a distance where the outside edges of the stakes match the width of the tray. Cut the third stake into four struts that match the gap between the first two stakes. Nail the struts into place. It not only gives rigid support, but will also provide convenient carrying handles and improve drainage.
3. Collect a range of trees of varying species, ages and sizes that suit the design. For under-plantings and bush effects, collect seedling trees, ferns or heather.

Various specimens brought together for the landscape planting

RIGHT: Rocks and moss gathered for the planting

BELOW: Work from a sketch of the finished landscape

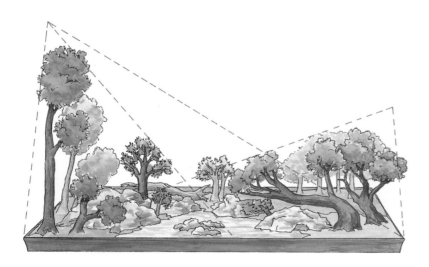

4. Collect rocks, all of the same colour and type of stone.
5. Make a sketch of where each tree will fit into the landscape to indicate how it should be pruned to shape.
6. Put the tray on its support frame and cover the bottom of the tray with gravel.
7. The 'hard' landscaping should be done first. Put the rocks in place. For realism, ensure that any fault lines run in the same direction, and place the largest rock at the front in order to create perspective.

LEFT: *Laying out the rocks*

RIGHT: *The trees and rocks loosely in position for detailed assessment*

LEFT: *Cutting back roots and long branches*

Trees planted and wired into place, and rocks firmly in position

BELOW: *The landscape a few weeks after planting, with under-plantings, driftwood and gravel all in place*

8. Select the trees that are to be dominant in the planting and those that are to be towards the rear of the landscape. Take them out of their pots and cut back the roots and any over-long branches. Do not take off too many branches at this stage, as they may be needed later.

9. Place all the trees loosely in position and assess the overall look of the landscape. When transposed from paper to the tray, any design faults will become evident and further rocks, plants and tree might be needed to make the landscape look 'right'.

10. Once a firm decision has been made over the position of each tree, plant it firmly and wire it into place. Cover the roots with appropriate compost and add the ancillary under-plantings of ferns, driftwood, and so on.

11. Water the planting thoroughly until water comes through the drainage holes and place on the bonsai bench or balcony.

12. After a few weeks it might be apparent that some of the trees are either not flourishing or may need to be replaced for other reasons. Replace the trees as necessary.

13. Maintain the landscape by keeping it free from weeds and cutting back any foliage that grows too rapidly and threatens to dwarf its neighbours.

Creating the slab: after attaching the fibreglass to the wire it should be folded with the join 'underneath' the slab

Project 4

Aim: *to make an artificial rock slab*

Materials:
Glass-fibre material, double the size of the intended slab
High-alumina cement (cement fondue)
Fencing wire (small-mesh chicken wire is ideal), double the size of the intended slab
Mixing bowl and spoon
Wire-cutters or tin snips
Paintbrush
Mist-sprayer
Twine or knitting yarn
Large needle

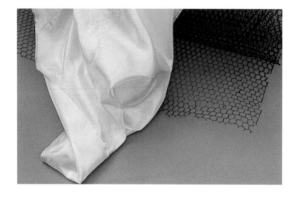

Glass-fibre material and small-mesh chicken wire

Method:

1. Select a glass-fibre material, either glass-fibre tissue, glass-fibre matting or woven glass-fibre material. Woven material is the easiest to use and attach to the chicken wire.

2. Cut the glass-fibre material and the chicken wire to the same size. As they both have to be folded in half, double the width or length of the intended slab is needed.

3. Attach the glass-fibre material to the chicken wire. The more fixing points there are, the greater definition of shape can be achieved. Sewing the material to the chicken wire with twine is a quick and easy way of joining the two.

4. Fold the wire in half, with the join down the middle of the back, so that it is out of sight. Fix the join by sewing the sides together. When fixed, turn it over so that the join is underneath the 'slab' (*see* above).

5. Start to bend the slab into shape. If the two sides become difficult to move, lever them apart with a screwdriver. Choose a shape to suit the purpose. For a group planting, a flat surface is required and a shape rather like a shallow canoe. If the slab is for a large rugged tree, depth is needed and the construction should be more of a 'shoe' shape.

6. When the overall shape has been achieved, spray it with water as a base for the cement mixture.

7. A slab larger than 3ft (90cm) long will need an internal structure to give it support. A metal bar or a length of wood will serve this purpose.

8. Mix the cement in small quantities, as it thickens very quickly. Put the cement in the bowl and add water to it until a thick, creamy consistency is achieved.

9. Cover the structure with cement mixture, front and back.

10. When the first coat is dry, inspect the slab thoroughly inside and out to ensure that no

BELOW: Stitching the chicken wire to the glass-fibre material with twine

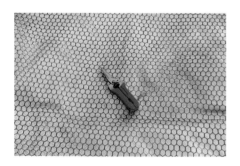

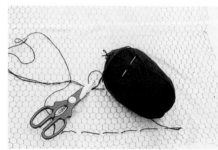

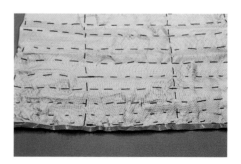

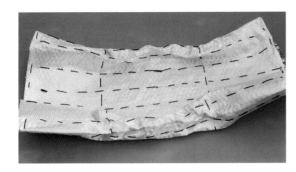

TOP LEFT: *Start to bend the wire into shape*

MIDDLE LEFT: *For a larger tree, a 'shoe' shape is more appropriate*

LOWER LEFT: *Mixing the cement*

TOP AND SECOND RIGHT: *The slab covered on all sides*

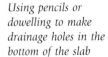

Using pencils or dowelling to make drainage holes in the bottom of the slab

The finished slab with compost, grit and retaining wires in place

parts have been missed. Push dowelling or pencils through the bottom of the slab to create drainage holes.

11. Several coats of cement will be necessary to give a rigid construction. The cement dries very quickly, so another coat may be added after a few hours.

12. The cement dries to a mid-grey colour so add a cement colorant or acrylic paint to the final coat of cement if another colour effect is desired. It is impossible to tell what colour the mixture will dry so try it out on the base of the slab before applying it to the top.

13. Allow the slab to harden before planting on it. Brush it down to remove debris and loose cement and rub it over with a bit of manure to encourage moss and lichens to attach themselves.

16 Case Histories

General Principles

The trees in this chapter have been included not because they were good but because, frankly, they were awful. They were developed from garden-centre trees, collected seedlings and field-grown material and, either through natural faults or inexperienced pruning, all but one were very nearly relegated to the compost heap. However, with patience and tenacity, the trees are now becoming quite presentable.

All beginners have had some problems with trees and this section demonstrates that you should never give up on your failures, as ugly ducklings can turn into trainee swans.

Birch Group

Years One to Three of Training

The seven seedling birch trees that made up this group were collected while on a walking holiday in Scotland and were potted individually. About three years later they were put together on a drilled drainage saucer. Perspective was lost because the dominant tree was at the back of the group rather than at the front. Two years later, the group was moved on to another drainage saucer and further rocks were added.

Years Five to Eight of Training

The group was re-planted on to a home-made freestyle ceramic pot and was converted into a landscape, with the addition of a pathway. The whole planting was still less than 12in (30cm) high but the trunks needed thickening in relation to the branches. Three years later (year eight), the group was planted in a totally unsuitable deep pot. Unchecked growth took place,

Birch group – years one to three of training

150

TOP, MIDDLE AND
LOWER LEFT: *Birch
group – years five to
eight of training*

RIGHT: *Birch group –
year ten of training*

land. Given another decade or so, the group should resemble the hill-grown birches of Cumbria.

Chinese Elm

Years One to Three of Training

*Chinese Elm – years
one to three of training*

which introduced character into the trunks and more thickness in the branches.

Year Ten of Training

Ten years down the line from the start of training, and thirteen years from collection, all the trees were alive and still less than 12in (30cm) tall. The trees were moved on to an artificial slab, and rocks, moss and gravel paths were added to create an atmosphere of hillside wood-

This was a field-grown tree that had been cut back from a larger tree. The top had taper but there was very little growth on the branches, and there were very ugly crossing roots. It should not have been planted in a bonsai pot at this stage but should have been put in a larger pot so that it could make growth. The lowest branch had been allowed to extend to several feet long, to encourage it to thicken.

By year three, the branches were still very spindly and there had been excessive growth at the top of the tree. The foliage was looking healthy and the worst of the crossed roots had been eliminated during re-potting, but the tree still looked scrawny and unsightly.

By year six, the lower branches had thickened and the foliage was a healthy green. The roots had been further improved but the tree lacked shape and needed pruning into a more natural form, with the branches becoming progressively shorter higher up the trunk.

In year eight, the tree was acquiring character and a more pleasing shape. Shaping had been accomplished purely with selective pruning; no wire had been used on the tree. However, a more suitable pot needed to be found if it was to look like a mature tree.

Year Ten

Re-potting the tree into a shallow oval pot gave an illusion of greater thickness to the trunk and age to the tree. The tree still had a good taper and now had a promising future.

Years Six to Eight of Training

LEFT: Year six of training: branches have begun to thicken

BOTTOM LEFT: Year eight of training; after summer pruning

RIGHT: Chinese Elm – year ten of training

Corsican Pine

Years One to Three of Training

In its first year of training, this tree had just about everything possible wrong with it: T-bar branches, whorls of branches, straight stretches and a straight, spindly trunk. An abortive attempt had been made to induce some shape in the branches with the use of inappropriately thin garden wire. It did not look promising. The Corsican Pine does not have tidy, compact foliage so the tree always looks shaggy.

LEFT: *Corsican Pine –
years one (TOP) and
three (BOTTOM) of
training*

RIGHT: *Corsican Pine
– years four (TOP) and
six (BOTTOM) of
training*

on to a home-made artificial slab under-planted
with alpines. The tree had a windswept look but
had been planted in an upright position that
did not tell a convincing story. The root was
ugly and needed to be planted lower on the
slab as it had no real spread. Little attempt had
been made to wire the branches and twigs into
shape.

By year six, neglect had allowed the tree to
grow freely. Extensive long growth had
occurred, which needed to be shortened and
shaped.

By year three, some character was beginning
to form. The top of the tree had been removed,
leaving two unfortunate eye-poking *jins*.
However, the branches were developing and the
worst of the whorls of branches had been eliminated.

Years Four and Six

A year on, the tree still had the same basic shape
but had made some growth, having been moved

Year Eight

The tree had been re-potted on to the same artificial slab with more slant. Next time the tree is
re-potted, this slant will be increased further
until a more windswept aspect is achieved. After
pruning back of all of the over-long shoots,
back-budding has occurred and the tree will
now develop more density. The roots of the tree
have been spread and it has been planted more
deeply. The roots 'downwind' of the tree will be
encouraged to thicken and be more exposed,

Corsican Pine – year eight of training

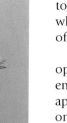

giving the effect that they are buttressing the tree against the elements. The eye-poking *jins* at the top of the tree have been removed and the tree now shows promise.

Mugo Pine – Mountain Pine

Years One to Three of Training

The tree was about six years old when it started its first year of training as a bonsai. It was developed from a garden-centre tree and was chosen because of its neat foliage. As usual with beginners, the tree had a flat look.

Photographs of bonsai trees give a distorted view of the tree and, as the back branches tend to be obscured by the trunk, novice bonsai growers often cut them off in error instead of developing them. There were no ugly T-bar branches but, as there had been only a very

minimal application of thin wire, the tree was totally lacking in character. It looked exactly what it was – a sapling tree that had had some of its branches cut off.

By year three, as the grower's skills developed, wire had been applied to the trunk, encouraging it to bend. No wire had been applied to the side branches. A middle branch on the right-hand side had been removed and a small, misplaced *jin* had been created.

Years Five to Seven of Training

The tree had made some vigorous growth and the branches had started to fill out. However, the top of the tree had acquired a pom-pom effect and the trunk was still spindly. At some time over the next couple of years the top of the tree was removed, leaving just one small

RIGHT: *Mugo Pine – years five to seven of training; by year five, the tree had acquired a pom-pom effect (TOP); by year seven, the top of the tree had been removed and wire had been added to the branches (LOWER)*

LEFT AND MIDDLE: *Mugo Pine – years one to three of training; by year three (MIDDLE), wire had been applied to the trunk*

LEFT: *Mugo Pine – years nine to eleven of training; by year eleven, feeding had led to extensive growth of candles (BELOW)*

Mugo Pine – year twelve of training; at eighteen years of age, the tree may now be termed a bonsai

shoot to act as a new leader. Wire had been added to the branches to spread the twigs and create character, but the tree looked awful and was nearly discarded.

Years Nine to Eleven

The tree had been moved into a larger oval pot in which it was thriving. The new leader had started to form an apex to the tree and extensive back budding had occurred after pruning of the trunk. Small side-shoots were now forming branches and the tree had improved rapidly. As the tree was fed regularly, abundant spring growth was evident in the extent of the candles.

Year Twelve

Now the tree is about eighteen years old, and has style and character. The trunk has thickened over the years and extensive back-budding has given a density of twigging and foliage to the lower branches. Almost every twig has been wired into shape. The tree now has possibilities and can be termed a bonsai. It is still in the same oval pot.

Final thoughts

Keeping bonsai soon becomes compulsive. Once you have learned to style your own trees, the one bonsai that you started off with quickly proliferates until you have many trees. Space will inevitably become a problem. Bonsai enthusiasts are always loath to part with any of their trees, but if you try to keep too large a number of trees, some are sure to suffer. Keep only the number of bonsai that you can maintain in the way that they should be maintained.

As you progress, your skills will develop and your confidence will grow. Experiment artistically but always remember that the tree is a living thing, and must be treated with respect. If you do this, it will reward you with hours of pleasure. Some of your trees will die. Be philosophical. If it was your fault, ensure that you don't make the same mistake again. If the cause of its demise was unknown, accept the loss as an act of nature and devote your attention to your remaining trees.

Happy snipping!

It's a hard life being a bonsai

Glossary of

Bonsai Terms

Accent planting Small flowering plants and grasses used to enhance the display of bonsai

Air layering The process by which roots are encouraged to form on a trunk, stem or branch

Akadama Imported clay used in bonsai composts

Alternate Relating to the position of leaves on a branch; leaves formed singly on the branch

Apex The top of the trunk of the tree

Baccatus Berry-forming

Back-budding Buds that form on old wood

Bunjingi Bonsai style – personal free-form style that is outside the rules

Cambium The layer of live wood that is under the bark, consisting of the phloem and the xylem

Chokkan Bonsai style – formal upright

Chumono Bonsai size – medium

Compound Relating to leaves – two or more leaflets

Cone Seed-bearing woody fruit

Conifer Cone-bearing tree

Cutting Small piece of severed branch that is rooted to form a new tree

Deciduous Trees that drop their leaves at the end of the growing season

Ericaceous Suitable for acid-loving plants

Evergreen Retaining leaves all year

Fukinagashi Bonsai style – windswept

Han-Kengai Bonsai style – semi-cascade

Hokidachi Bonsai style – broom, resembling a brush

Hortag Calcined clay lumps used for benching

Ikadabuki Bonsai style – raft planting (single tree laid flat with branches acting as trunks)

Inorganic Matter that has never been alive

Ishitsuki Bonsai style – root-on-rock, root clasped to rock

Jin Section of branch from which the bark has been removed

Kabudachi Bonsai style – root-connected clump. Several trunks coming from one root

Kengai Bonsai style – formal cascade

Keshitsubu Bonsai size – tiny trees that can fit into thimble-sized pots

Kobukan Bonsai style – knobbly trunk

Lime sulphur Solution used to whiten and preserve *jins* and *sharis*

Mame Bonsai size – very small (under 6in/15cm)

Moyogi Bonsai style – formal upright, straight trunk with the apex over the base of the trunk

Mycelium Fungus found around the roots of pines and oaks. Very beneficial to the tree

Ne Agari Bonsai style – exposed root

Nejikan Bonsai style – spiral trunk

Netsunagari Bonsai style – sinuous planting (trunks coming from one tree on its side but not forming a straight line)

Omono Bonsai size – large trees

Opposite Relating to the position of leaves on a branch; leaves in pairs

Organic Matter that was once alive

Palmate Relating to leaves; ribs radiating like outstretched fingers

Perlite   Natural mineral expanded by heat

Phloem   Part of the vascular system of food delivery in the tree

Photosynthesis   The process by which leaves produce food for the tree and release oxygen into the air

Pinching   Taking out the growing tips of shoots using a finger and thumb

Pinnate   Relating to leaves – of compound structure

Sabakan   Bonsai style – hollow trunk

Saikei   Bonsai style – landscape plantings

Scarifying   Breaking down the coat of a hard seed

Sekijoju   Bonsai style – root-over-rock

Shakan   Bonsai style – slanting

Sharamiki   Bonsai style – driftwood

Shari   Section of trunk from which bark has been removed

Shohin   Bonsai size – small trees

Sokan   Bonsai style – twin trunk

Stratification   Subjecting a seed to a period of cold to encourage it to germinate

Systemic   Chemical that works by being absorbed by the plant and acting through the sap

Tosho   Bonsai style – triple trunk (three trunks coming from one root)

Topiary   The art of pruning bushes and trees into unnatural shapes

Tufa   A porous stone formed from constantly dripping lime-rich water

Whorl   Three or more shoots or stems emerging from the same level on a branch

Wound sealant   A compound used to cover pruning cuts to prevent disease

Xylem   Part of the vascular system of the tree; delivers the raw materials of food production

Yose-Ue   Bonsai style – group plantings

Cut-Leaf Red Maple (Acer palmatum 'Dissectum Purpureum'): maples make wonderful bonsai material as they have a wide range of leaf shapes and colours. These leaves will turn brilliant orange in the autumn

Index